Capacity Planning for Internet Services

Quick Planning Techniques for High Growth Rates

Adrian Cockcroft
Bill Walker

Sun Microsystems Press
A Prentice Hall Title

The publisher offers discounts on this book when ordered in bulk quantities. For more information, contact: Corporate Sales Department, Phone: 800-382-3419; Fax: 201-236-7141; E-mail: corpsales@prenhall.com; or write: Prentice Hall PTR, Corp. Sales Dept., One Lake Street, Upper Saddle River, NJ 07458.

Editorial/production superviser: *Nicholas Radhuber*
Cover design director: *Jerry Votta*
Cover designer: *Kavish & Kavish Digital Publishing & Design*
Manufacturing manager: *Alexis R. Heydt*
Marketing manager: *Debby vanDijk*
Acquisitions editor: *Gregory G. Doench*

Sun Microsystems Press
Marketing manager: *Michael Llwyd Alread*
Publisher: *Rachel Borden*

10 9 8 7 6 5 4 3 2 1

ISBN 0-13-089402-8

Sun Microsystems Press
A Prentice Hall Title

Contents

Figures

Tables

Acknowledgments

Bill thanks Hattie Hall for her support and encouragement during the writing of this book.

During the training classes Adrian presented as part of the WICS program at Stanford University, he learned a great deal about capacity planning techniques from Dr. Neil Gunther. Members of the Computer Measurement Group, especially those at the meetings in the United States, Australia, and Italy, provided inspiration and ideas that span the UNIX® and mainframe-oriented worlds. Dave Fisk provided detailed feedback on the disk capacity estimation section. Many thanks to all those who listened and provided feedback during presentations.

Dave Blankenhorn provided a detailed discussion of Service Level Agreements that was incorporated into the principles and processes chapters.

SunPS℠ talent and the SunReady™ team were instrumental in helping Bill put his thoughts into words and acting as a sounding board for ideas. Our express thanks to Jean-Marc Bernard, Brian Carter, Jefre Futch, and Jeffrey Lucove for their help.

Ken Pepple coauthored our technical seminar series on performance management, which was used as a framework for the principles chapter. Jason Fish provided the organizational talent for the technical seminars, and helped fill classrooms around the world. Bill Bishop and Tom Bankert gave us the latitude to pursue this area in depth, and to spend the time refining the seminar and writing this book.

Thanks to David Deeths for the detailed technical review and modifications that were instrumental in getting this book completed.

Many thanks to Barbara Jugo for project management and to Terry Williams for editing this book.

Preface

The Sun BluePrints™ series provides best practices information in book form for the users of Sun™ products. The series looks at the combination of techniques and methodologies of assembling Sun and third-party products that are needed to solve real-world problems and business needs.

Capacity Planning for Internet Services provides detailed yet concise recipes for performing capacity planning tasks for high-growth-rate Internet services. It assumes that there is very little time or expertise available to perform these tasks.

Who Should Use This Book

This Sun BluePrints book is primarily intended for Capacity Planners, Operations Managers, Systems and Database Administrators, Systems Integrators, and Systems Engineers. It can be used as a first introduction to the subject of capacity planning and performance management in an Internet-oriented environment. The techniques described are quite generic, and the only areas of this book that are Sun specific relate to understanding some of the measurements available on the Sun platform. It does not assume any background in capacity planning and avoids the detailed mathematics of queueing theory as much as possible. However, many references are provided for advanced reading.

How This Book Is Organized

The two authors of this book bring together a wide variety of experiences to provide a practical but innovative guide to the problems of capacity planning in high-growth-rate Internet environments. Adrian Cockcroft is a Distinguished Systems Engineer at Sun and is well-known for his expertise and many presentations on performance tuning and tools. Adrian initiated this writing project, structured and scoped the book, and is primarily responsible for the *Scenario Planning* and *Observability* chapters. Bill Walker is one of the most senior members of Sun's Professional Services℠ (SunPS℠) organization. He has worked on many large Internet sites, currently designs processes and methodologies for the SunPS team to implement, and regularly presents training classes on performance tuning. Bill is primarily responsible for the *Capacity Estimation, Suggested Processes*, and *Tools Overview and Evaluations* chapters.

Chapter 1, "Introduction," is an overview of the reasons why this Sun BluePrints series was written and a description of the problems it tries to address.

Chapter 2, "Theoretical Principles," explains some of the underlying principles involved in managing high growth rates and in making trade-offs between conflicting requirements.

Chapter 3, "Suggested Processes," describes how to implement processes and procedures for establishing service level agreements and performing capacity planning.

Chapter 4, "Scenario Planning," introduces a simple way to identify your primary bottleneck, perform capacity estimation, define future scenarios, and perform spreadsheet-based capacity planning.

Chapter 5, "Capacity Estimation," describes how to examine CPU, memory, disks, and networks to determine the capacity available and the utilization of that capacity. A closer examination of the problems in obtaining capacity and utilization for bottleneck estimation is also presented.

Chapter 6, "Observability," looks at the reporting requirements for a site in terms of the needs of operations, engineering, and senior management.

Chapter 7, "Tools Overview and Evaluations" looks at the many tools available for capacity planning, and contains a detailed look at the TeamQuest tools that the SunPS team uses to perform capacity planning studies.

Appendix A, "Sun Constant Performance Metrics," provides Sun Constant Performance Metrics (SCPM) estimation tables for Sun servers.

Appendix B, "References," provides a list of publications and Web sites for finding out about more advanced techniques, and contacting tool vendors.

Related Books

These books provide relevant background material; for full details and more suggestions, see the references in Appendix B.

- The Sun BluePrints OnLine Web site: http://www.sun.com/blueprints/online.html
- *The Practical Performance Analyst* by Dr. Neil Gunther
- *Configuration and Capacity Planning for Sun Servers* by Brian Wong

- *Sun Performance and Tuning – Java and the Internet* by Adrian Cockcroft and Richard Pettit
- *Resource Management*, a Sun BluePrints book by Richard McDougall, Adrian Cockcroft, Evert Hoogendoorn, Tom Bialaski, and Enrique Vargas
- *Solaris PC Netlink Performance, Sizing, and Deployment*, a Sun BluePrints book by Don DeVitt
- *Backup and Restore Practices for Sun Enterprise Servers,* a Sun BluePrints book by Stan Stringfellow and Miroslav Klivansky, with Michael Barto

For a list of Sun documents and how to order them, see the catalog section of the SunExpress™ Internet site at http://www.sun.com/sunexpress

How to Access Sun Documentation Online

The docs.sun.com Web site enables you to access Sun technical documentation online. You can browse the docs.sun.com archive or search for a specific book title or subject. The URL is http://docs.sun.com/.

What Typographic Changes Mean

TABLE P-1 describes the typographic changes used in this book.

TABLE P-1   Typographic Conventions

Typeface or Symbol	Meaning	Example
AaBbCc123	The names of commands, files, and directories; on-screen computer output	Edit your.login file. Use ls -a to list all files. machine_name% You have mail.
AaBbCc123	What you type, contrasted with on-screen computer output	machine_name% **su** Password:
AaBbCc123	Command-line placeholder; replace with a real name or value	To delete a file, type rm *filename*.
AaBbCc123	Book titles, new words or terms, or words to be emphasized	Read Chapter 6 in *User's Guide*. These are called *class* options. You *must* be root to do this.

Shell Prompts in Command Examples

TABLE P-2 shows the default system prompt and superuser prompt for the C shell, Bourne shell, and Korn shell.

TABLE P-2   UNIX Shell Prompts

Typeface or Symbol	Meaning
C shell prompt	`machine_name%`
C shell superuser prompt	`machine_name#`
Bourne shell and Korn shell prompt	`$`
Bourne shell and Korn shell superuser prompt	`#`

CHAPTER 1

Introduction

Almost every business, from a corner shop to a multinational corporation, is faced with competitive pressure to "go online" and provide services via an Internet site. In addition, a large number of new online businesses are being implemented in a mad dash to capture the attention and wallets of a huge and fast-growing number of Internet users. Success is measured by growth in the number of pages viewed, registered users, and in some cases, by the amount of business transacted.

Success comes at a cost. Rapid growth can overwhelm the ability of the site to provide services with acceptable performance. There have been many reports of Web sites that have suddenly attracted too many users and collapsed under the strain.

Startup dot-com companies spend most of their investors' funds on advertising as they attempt to establish their name in the collective consciousness of consumers and the media. Established companies are concerned about maintaining their preexisting brand image while gaining credibility as they add Internet services to their traditional businesses. Therefore, it is important to provide enough capacity to cope with sudden increases in load.

Traditional computer installations have a relatively static number of users, and a detailed understanding of their workload patterns can be obtained. Growth rates in this environment are relatively low, and costs can be optimized by careful capacity planning. Internet services are available to many millions of potential users of the service. The load on the service depends upon the whim of the users. If a high-profile advertisement or news item reaches a large number of people, there is a great opportunity to expand the user base as long as the site can cope with the load. Growth rates for successful sites in this environment are very high, and very hard to plan for. It is normal to lurch from one crisis to the next and to throw hardware quick fixes at the problem regardless of the cost.

Capacity planning is an optimization process. Service level requirements can be predicted and balanced against their costs. Even if there are few cost constraints, it is important to have good estimates of how much spare capacity the site has and whether it can survive the next load peak.

Capacity planning is a well-known discipline, particularly for sites that have a mainframe-oriented background. When very high growth rates occur, time constraints prevent normal techniques from being applied. This Sun BluePrints book charts a course through the available techniques and tools; examines time scales and return on investment for different methodologies; provides a framework for decomposing big problems into solvable subproblems; and gives simple, practical examples that provide results in hours thanks to spreadsheet-based techniques. If you wait until you have chosen and purchased an expensive tool, you will then need weeks or months to learn how to use it. These tools are useful and powerful, and their use is also described in detail.

The topics covered in this book can be divided into the following sections:

- Principles and processes
- Scenario planning techniques
- The effective use of tools

Compared to conventional capacity planning techniques, the Internet service capacity planning techniques described in this book must cope with high rates of change, work with limited system administrator experience, and steer a path through confusing choices and a lack of tools.

Because there are also increased availability requirements, it is important to give priority to simple, common-sense principles that can be followed consistently.

CHAPTER 2

Theoretical Principles

With the exponential growth of the Internet and consumer electronic commerce on the Internet, service quality has become a key component of success. Electronic commerce and commercial portals on the Internet expose the business front office and the related business back office systems to scrutiny by the direct consumer, as well as by the news media.

Sun servers have entered the traditional datacenter environment where system availability, manageability, and service availability are key components in providing a solution to business requirements. With an established and encompassing "production environment" life-cycle plan, robust solutions can be safely and reliably placed into production and evolved to meet the changing and growing needs of the business.

This chapter presents methods for managing performance and establishing service level agreements (SLAs). It also examines the IT frameworks designed to provide solutions for production environment business requirements. Additional IT frameworks from ISO FCAPS (fault, configuration, application, performance, and security) models are presented, and tips are offered for implementation.

Performance Management

Performance management is the measurement, analysis, and optimization of computer resources to provide an agreed-upon level of service to the end-user. By defining performance management and identifying the key components required to safely and accurately implement performance management in the datacenter, you can minimize the risks associated with high growth rates. These risks include:

- System downtime due to unexpected overload
- Negative customer feedback
- Loss of potential business due to poor response times
- Loss of customer loyalty due to perceived lack of service quality

The key components that we will concentrate on to define our scope of performance management will include:

- Throughput
- Latency
- Utilization

Throughput is defined as the number of defined actions performed in a given period of time. *Latency* is defined as the time that it takes to complete a well-defined action

Throughput and latency can be applied at a high level while measuring transactions at the end-user level. They can also be examined for discrete events such as network packets, disk activity, or system centerplane bandwidth consumption. Each of these levels of detail can be measured, reported, and analyzed for impact on overall system performance, provided that you understand the events being monitored and the capabilities of the resources involved in providing those actions.

Utilization is usually expressed as the percentage of the overall capability of a given resource consumed during a defined action or quantity of actions. Resource utilization and resource utilization planning are the cornerstones of capacity planning. Utilization is a measure of system resource impact, throughput defines the quantity of services, and latency defines the quality of the services being provided.

; of Service Architecture

Several layers of resources and resource consumption can be defined, tuned, measured, and reported within the service architecture. Categorizing these layers (see TABLE 2-1) and defining the expectations for each level provides the guidelines for the design and implementation of a system.

TABLE 2-1   Layers of Service Architecture

Layer	Components
Business	Number of users Batch job definitions Report schedules Business hours
Application	N-tiered architecture Database layout Software architecture Access methods
Operating System	Kernel tuning OS revisions Disk volume layouts
Hardware	CPU Disk Memory
Infrastructure	Network architecture Enterprise management Backup strategies

Each of these layers of the overall service architecture affords opportunities for tuning, measurement, reporting, and management. Each layer will have its own particular scale of benefit and investment to introduce change.

The Business layer often provides the most significant opportunities for "tuning" and has the most significant contribution to the overall architecture. The Application layer and Hardware layer can also provide a significant and obvious impact on the overall performance of the architecture. The Operating System and Infrastructure layers are often where administrators look for some magic cure, but these layers often provide the least opportunity for impacting the performance of a system.

Phases of Performance Management

Performance management can be applied in an iterative, cyclic, four-phase approach (see FIGURE 2-1).

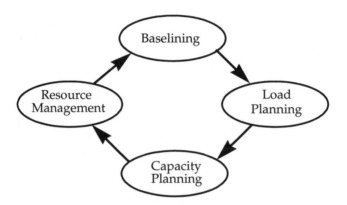

FIGURE 2-1 Four-Phase Approach to Performance Management

The output of each phase is used as input to the following phase. Each phase must reach a steady state in which the results can be published and transferred to the following phase. Once the four phases are locked in place and all results have been published, those results are fed into the next generation of phases. The next sections discuss each phase in detail.

A relatively simple change and configuration management process integrated into the performance management deliverables can greatly improve the efficiency and accuracy of performance management. This change management can be as simple as generating and maintaining revision numbers for the documentation and reports that are produced.

Historical revisions should be retained for future examination and change analysis. These revisions also provide a history of changes to the data analyzed and the resulting conclusions. This compilation of historic data and conclusions can help reduce repetition of effort and acts as a guide that displays the impacts (both positive and negative) of past load planning and capacity planning.

Baselining

Baselining creates a snapshot of a system as it currently exists and generates reports that describe the system performance and the characterization of the workload being measured. To baseline a system, we first describe the goals of system performance in throughput, latency, and utilization within each level of the service architecture.

The business requirements of the service being provided by the established workload must first be defined. These end-user service level requirements can include:

■ Transaction rates

■ Transactional volumes

■ Hours of operation

■ Critical time frames for processing batch loads

■ Concurrent user session requirements

These are the same business requirements defined in the SLA, which is explained in detail in Chapter 3, "Suggested Processes."

A configuration inventory establishes a record of the current state of the five layers of the service architecture and provides a reference for modifying that architecture. An accurate representation including hardware, software, and operating system versions is critical to creating an accurate inventory. This configuration inventory is considered "locked down" for the life span of the baselining process. This causes all changes to the operating environment to be considered a tuning event that expires the current system state and triggers a new baselining cycle.

At this point, service performance is monitored and measured against the goals defined in the SLA. In addition, system performance is monitored and measured against the desired resource consumption thresholds defined in the key performance indicator (KPI) document, as addressed in Chapter 3.

If any tuning opportunities are identified in any of the five layers of system performance, the identified changes to the system or architecture are implemented and remeasured against the previous snapshot. This helps to determine the positive or negative effects of those changes on system performance. The old snapshot is retained as a historical record of configuration and resulting performance metrics, and the new snapshot becomes the working baseline.

Load Planning

Load planning accounts for changes or new demands on the system. Any available data describing the changes and new demands is collected and analyzed. If possible, measurements are taken by baselining similar workloads or workloads in the development phase. The new workloads or changes to the existing workloads are profiled, providing input to the capacity planning phase (see FIGURE 2-2).

Load Planning is a cyclical process that comprises three activities: load assessment, load data gathering, and load profiling. Each of these activities may need to be repeated multiple times before valid assumptions can be made about the data collected.

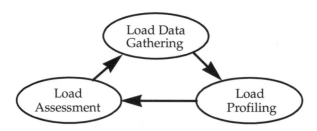

FIGURE 2-2   Load Planning

Load Assessment identifies how the new demand can be quantified. In the case of a new pool of end-users migrating to an application, *load assessment* would determine where the users would be located, how they would be accessing the environment, what they would be doing in the environment, and the frequency with which they would do it. This information could then drive the creation of benchmarks to test the effects of this new demand on the existing environment.

Load Data Gathering collects raw statistics on the transactions within a benchmark. This collection can be accomplished in many ways depending on the layer that is focused on. These statistics tend to be much more detailed and over shorter intervals than those measured during baselining activities. These measurements usually take place in an isolated development environment or test environment.

Load Profiling creates a model based on the load-gathering data. This model will represent the typical load that is applied to a system for that particular planning cycle.

Capacity Planning

Capacity planning applies the results of the load planning analysis to the system baseline and performance reports from the baselining phase. The capacity planning phase produces a new system and service configuration architecture to meet the requirements established in the load planning phase. The accuracy of the data collected in the baselining and load planning phases is directly related to the accuracy of the capacity planning model.

System capacity and resource consumption are modelled, calibrated, and validated against the current baseline data. The model compares the relative resource consumptions (measured in the performance reports of the baselining process) to the relative performance characteristics of the system architecture (established during the configuration inventory of the baselining process). The relationship between resource consumption and system architecture capabilities creates the workload characterization used to model and predict the effect of changes (deltas) to the measured environment.

System performance characteristics are established and projected into a model of scenarios that include projected workload growth, system architecture and hardware changes, and workload resource assignment.

Once the model has been established as accurate and representative of the measured workload characteristics, the model is used to predict the impact of the changes introduced in the load planning phase. The operating environment can be adjusted as necessary to meet the established performance requirements defined in the SLA and KPI.

Application disk layouts, disk architecture models, CPU speeds, cache sizes, memory sizing, and workload mixes can be adjusted and projected in the system model. The new workload is projected into the new system environment in an iterative process until a system environment that meets the business requirements and performance objectives is found. This iterative process produces utilization, latency, and throughput projections for the new workload, as well as a system architecture and operating environment that meet the planned changes and growth while maintaining a predictable level of service to the end-user community.

Resource Management

Resource management defines the controls, shares, quotas, and priorities necessary to manage the workload within the implemented production environment. Shares and quotas are enforced and monitored for accounting where necessary. In addition, system resource accounting provides input for creating the new baseline of system performance. System resource planning also provides additional calibration feedback into the next phase of load planning and capacity planning to improve model accuracy. Refer to the Sun BluePrints book *Resource Management* for an exhaustive view of resource management.

Service Level Agreements

With the increasing performance and RAS (reliability, availability, and serviceability) of Sun servers and software, Solaris™ Operating Environment, or Solaris OE-based servers have been encroaching on what has traditionally been the mainframe world of mission-critical applications. This relatively new positioning of Sun servers in the enterprise has resulted in the necessity for IT departments to apply mainframe disciplines to UNIX servers. One of the staples in the mainframe environment that is still relatively new to the Solaris OE is the service level agreement (SLA). These agreements outline the level of availability of mission-critical services between the IT department and end-users.

This section describes the principles of an SLA; the section "Service Level Management" on page 26 outlines the steps that IT departments should take in the analysis of the end-users' computing resource requirements, capabilities of the IT architecture, and formulation of the agreement.

The SLA is really just a list of *expectations* for a given service. Moreover, it is a tool for maintaining service availability. It defines the transactional capabilities, network latency projections, availability requirements, maintenance windows, escalation procedures, and the review process for those services.

When service levels are not explicitly defined, users will be left on their own to formulate their own idea of service levels. All too often, the service levels that the users create on their own will not correspond to those of the IT department. The unfortunate impacts of not establishing service levels are miscommunication and chaos. If proper communication does not take place between the provider and consumer, the SLA may be seen as a weapon to be used between the two parties, thereby negating proper communications and negotiations.

When used properly, the SLA becomes a bridge of understanding between the IT department and the service consumers. These agreements should be used as a basis of understanding between all parties involved and should define key roles, responsibilities, and expectations that have been discussed and agreed upon by all parties. Furthermore, the SLA should be reviewed and modified regularly and considered a living document. Any proposed modifications should be discussed and agreed to by all parties, before inclusion in the SLA.

In most established computing environments such as more traditional datacenters, SLAs have long been a staple of life. However, in the client/server world, the introduction of SLAs usually poses a significant cultural change. Usually, in this situation, the traditional technologically focused management needs to give way to management based on user satisfaction.

The SLA should answer five critical questions:

- What expectations do the users have for the service?
- What expectations do the providers have for the service?
- What do the users expect from the service provider (IT department)?
- What does the service provider expect from the users?
- How can the SLA improve the business process, affect the bottom line, and improve availability?

The answers to these questions may seem deceptively simple, but in reality, they may take months of negotiation to work out.

Nonexistent or poorly defined SLAs can result in many unpleasantries, not the least of which are:

- The perception of poor service because the IT department fails to meet the undocumented expectations of end-users
- Antagonistic work relationships between end-users and IT staff
- IT staff providing unwanted support, most likely at a price that the end-user is unwilling to pay (downside of this perception is that the IT department may be "looking for work" and thus become a target for new budget constraints)
- Inconsistent support and the possible impression of favoritism between the IT staff and end-users

Caveats and Problems with Service Level Agreements

SLAs are not more widely used for a number of reasons. Some of the most common are derived from the lack of end-user communication and the culture changes for IT departments. However, the many long-term benefits of SLAs include increased end-user satisfaction, more accurate resource accounting, and more efficient prioritization. The following issues are the most common downfalls of SLAs:

- IT department and end-user management did not commit substantial time and personnel.
- Lines of communication between IT department and end-user community were not established.

- IT managers could not concisely define, qualify, and quantify IT services and costs.
- IT managers lacked the marketing skills to identify, price, and sell IT services, both internally and externally.
- End-users did not know exactly what they wanted or when they wanted it.
- IT department failed to set baselines and run benchmarks on existing services and caused inaccurate predictions about future services.
- SLAs were not realistic and caused tested numbers to fail.

However, with the right IT skills, either from the internal IT department or external consulting organizations, all of these hurdles can be overcome.

The creation of the first SLA can be a challenging task for any IT department. It requires a new look at the service, which is largely from the end-user's perspective and can be a difficult cultural change.

However, the payoff of establishing and maintaining an SLA is well worth the effort for several reasons. A well-conveyed SLA can help develop higher service availability, greater end-user satisfaction, and more efficient use of computing resources. In addition, preferable control over IT budgets and increased accuracy in long-term budgeting can also be direct benefits of SLAs.

Further, the framework created by the SLA, based on input from the end-users and IT department, provides a number of benefits to IT management. With the SLA, an IT manager can assign personnel to requirements more effectively. Thus, personnel restrictions, whether due to staffing or skill limitations, can be addressed through hiring or training. This framework also provides insight into the coordination required to optimize enterprise IT spending, reinvestment, and priorities. This insight consequently reveals the link between IT service delivery and costs incurred for that service.

Production Environment Engineering

Successful production environment implementations are the product of careful planning and design. Production environment engineering and the topic of datacenter production environments have been studied and analyzed for decades. Balancing the business objectives, the explosive growth of Internet business, and the integrity and safety of the critical business services can certainly be classified as an art.

This section addresses the needs of the datacenter production environment by using the ISO FCAPS model, the ITIL (information technology infrastructure library) framework, a basic IT reference model, and the SunReady roadmap to production.

This discussion provides an encompassing view of the infrastructure requirements and timelines necessary to successfully launch, manage, and maintain a new datacenter service or refresh an existing one.

Overview

Traditional "glass house" datacenter managers are generally familiar with the concepts of production environment standards for operational policies and procedures, but are unprepared for the exponential growth experienced by the fast-paced dot-com consumer markets. These glass house managers must learn to:

- Adapt to the fast-paced Internet economy
- Be prepared to quickly accommodate the new model of instantaneous and direct customer contact
- Conform to an environment where exponential growth has become a standard in successful ventures

They must also realize that the traditional model of multi-layered sales and distribution retail markets is being challenged by the new access model that includes direct interaction between the corporate IT systems and the customer, with competition just a mouse click away.

The dot-com startup Internet business has a related challenge. While their business model relies on exponential growth for survival in the highly competitive Internet business environment, they often lack the datacenter policies, procedures, and experience to manage a datacenter production environment through the growth that some successful Internet businesses have displayed in recent years. By learning from the cumulative experience of their more traditional predecessors, the dot-com companies can implement best practices for the production environment architecture, while retaining the flexibility necessary to thrive in the expanding market.

IT Frameworks

An IT framework defines the scope of coverage in the production environment and consists of generalized topics to be designed and implemented in that environment. Frameworks also help determine staffing and organizational requirements based on broad categories of IT services. Examples of some traditional topics include:

- Backup and restore
- Change control
- Security
- Performance/capacity management

- System management
- Application management
- Network management
- Disaster recovery
- Facilities management

Some of the categories defined in the framework are company-wide, some are datacenter-specific, some are system-specific, and others are application-specific. For example, the security group could manage security policy and administration for the entire company, while a facilities management resource could be designated to several disparate datacenters. In addition, the application management resource could be dedicated to a single server or a set of service instances throughout multiple datacenters.

The ISO FCAPS IT Framework

The International Organization for Standardization (ISO) defined a framework for managed objects in a networked enterprise in their *Guidelines for the Definition of Managed Objects* contained in the *Open Systems Interconnection (OSI): Structure of Management Information* standard. The OSI structure defined five categories of managed objects, covering the basic categories of enterprise support operations (see FIGURE 2-3).

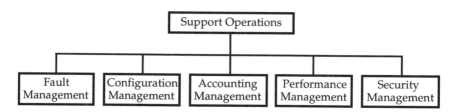

FIGURE 2-3　FCAPS High-Level IT Framework

These categories can be applied to network management systems, which is the intended purpose, or they can be expanded to include the skills, tools, and capabilities in datacenter operations and management.

IT Extended Frameworks

Each of the categories in an IT framework can be broken down into smaller pieces, describing the responsibilities of the group providing the service associated with that category. This expanded list of IT capabilities is called the IT extended framework (ITEF). TABLE 2-2 shows an example.

TABLE 2-2 IT Extended Framework

Fault Management
Customer Service
Incident Management
Backup and Recovery
Disaster Recovery
System Administration
Fault Protection

The ITEF provides an excellent checklist for datacenter capabilities, skill sets, and product coverage. It also provides a framework for establishing a logical structure for datacenter policies and procedures that is independent of operating system, server type, or application type. Several levels of criticality can be assigned to the categories of IT services established by the ITEF, such as mission-critical, business-critical, business support, and incidental. These levels of criticality can help determine the level of IT support needed for a particular category.

An ITEF can be further divided to establish functional responsibilities and to provide more detailed information about the services the ITEF offers. These functional responsibilities either can be represented as a table of departmental responsibilities (see TABLE 2-3) or they can be explicitly declared in an IT service coverage document defining departmental responsibilities.

TABLE 2-3 FCAPS IT Extended Framework Subdivision

Backup and Recovery
Tape Pool Management
User Data Restoration
System Backup
Data Backup Integrity Tests
Offsite Tape Archive Rotation

FCAPS IT Extended Framework

By expanding the FCAPS IT framework to include descriptive categories of IT service coverage, we can define an ITEF based on FCAPS. This ITEF is best represented in a tree structure that is viewable as a series of Web pages that allow the consumer to easily navigate to the level of detail needed. This drill-down structure is key for implementing the ITEF in an easily accessible shared presentation and for including the ITEF in online system runbooks.

FIGURE 2-4 shows the ISO FCAPS IT extended framework.

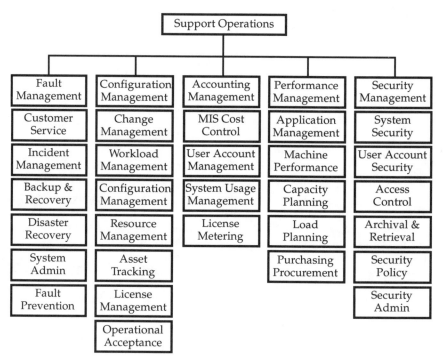

FIGURE 2-4   ISO FCAPS IT Extended Framework

A clear presentation of the logical architecture is important in presenting a unified IT management and operations strategy to both the end-user service consumer organizations and to business-level management. This presentation also helps enable accurate SLA creation and service capability interpretation. The following example provides an excerpt of a sample IT service coverage document for change management.

IT Service Coverage Document

The IT service coverage document should include a general statement describing the category of coverage, as well as including statements describing the individual services and areas of authority in the IT environment. The service coverage document can provide assistance in tool selection, as well as staffing and training requirements. By establishing categories of coverage, the services provided by the IT department are well-defined, which allows the establishment of enforcement and auditing policies across the IT operating environment.

Change Management

The change management system is the vehicle for *recording, authorizing, monitoring,* and *reporting* all changes to the open systems environment. The primary services and responsibilities provided are:

❑ *Single auditable mechanism for handling all changes integrated with the enterprise change management system*
❑ *Review process, including all interested parties, for authorizing changes*
❑ *Process for ensuring all changes are tested and validated with tested back-out procedures*
❑ *Change process reporting procedure incorporated within the SLA reporting process*
❑ *Mechanism for reviewing all changes not authorized through the change management procedure*
❑ *Control of software development and maintenance for applications and packages, including source code, executable code, and parameter files, plus the provision of release management and audit control*
❑ *Software distribution of applications, operating system, and packages to the distributed platforms in a controlled and audited manner*

The IT Service Model

The IT service model (ITSM) introduces levels of criticality, levels of service, and "big rules" to the ITEF. This multilevel approach extends the natural drill-down structure for IT services (see FIGURE 2-5).

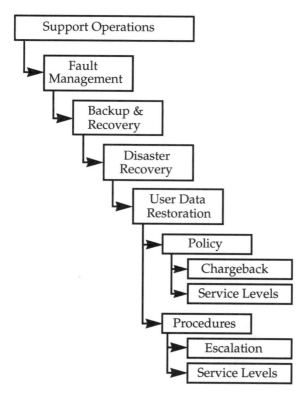

FIGURE 2-5   Drill-Down IT Document Hierarchy

The ITSM can be implemented across platforms and used to create service level descriptions for use in SLAs between end-user consumer organizations and IT resource provider organizations. Where appropriate, a chargeback structure for IT services can be produced for varying levels of service. Once defined, the ITSM helps produce an automated, standardized, repeatable, and simplified SLA creation and auditing process.

The following is a sample of a service level description for user data backup and can be used as a guideline; it should be modified to adhere to local datacenter policies.

Service:

User Data Backup

Service Schedule:

Maintenance Window Task

Service Levels:

Mission-Critical

User data will be backed up to the central backup management system using a full backup on a daily schedule.

Chargeback:

$1000 + $80 ÷ 100 GB per month

Business-Critical

User data will be backed up to the central backup management system with weekly full backups and daily incremental backups.

Chargeback:

$500 + $60 ÷ 100 GB per month

Business Support

User data will be backed up to a locally attached tape system with weekly full backups and daily incremental backups

Chargeback:

$200 + $40 ÷ 100 GB per month

Applying ITIL

The Central Computing and Telecommunication Agency (CCTA) of the UK began publishing volumes of their established best practices for IT operations in 1978. The 24 volumes, titled Information Technology Infrastructure Library (ITIL), describe the CCTA's operational procedures and discuss their application and logistics in a production datacenter environment.

The ITIL has evolved over the years, being studied, adopted, and adapted by many IT organizations and vendors of management tools. The Examination Institute of the Netherlands (EXIN) has established certification programs granting foundation, practitioner, and master levels of expertise to the categories of service support, service delivery, and IT management.

One key benefit of the ITIL is that it has helped identify the interdependencies inherent in IT management organizations. The following is an example of the interdependencies within a backup process:

1. Backups must first be scheduled through the batch job scheduling system.

2. The status and any errors of the backup must be reported through the enterprise monitoring and management system.

3. The monitoring and management system must transfer the status and any errors of the backup to the service desk.

4. The service desk must notify the technology owner or system administrator of the status and any errors.

With a properly organized IT framework and extended framework, these interdependencies and process flows can be documented. In addition, the procedures for implementation and operation can be integrated into the documentation describing the service.

The ITIL establishes policies, not implementations. It remains independent of operating system, hardware platform, and application, but can be used as a guideline for creating the "big rules" to be used in the ITEF. The ITEF can then be implemented according to service levels, operating system, hardware, and application capabilities.

Use the following resources to provide the knowledge necessary for implementation of the established policies in the ITEF:

- Sun BluePrints program

- Collective experience of the IT staff

- Technical publications and conferences

- Sun Education Services

- Sun Professional Services

The SunReady™ Approach

The FCAPS framework was originally generated from the ITIL. The Sun Professional Services (SunPS) team has developed a project methodology for applying the FCAPS framework. This methodology creates a unified extended framework for IT operations. Using the ITIL as a guideline for best practices in mission-critical environments, the SunPS team created sets of big rules for implementation. These rules weigh the criticality of each task required to deliver the service levels promised by the customer IT department to the end-users of the specified services.

By creating this multilevel approach to each IT service, the SunPS team can establish a scoring model to predict the ability of the current IT infrastructure to satisfy the requirements of the end-user service level objectives. This IT capability analysis can then be used to develop a high-level architecture for the IT infrastructure. This new, well-planned architecture can supplement the current established IT operations services before the end-user service is placed into production. Hence, the high-level architecture is optimally created before the pilot phase of the application development life cycle.

The implementation of supplemental service capabilities shadows the application development life cycle from the architecture phase to the pilot, development, integration, deployment, and sustaining phases. The IT service capabilities can then be tested and assessed simultaneously with the application's functional, stress, crash, and disaster recovery test cycles. In addition, the IT service capabilities can then be promoted into the live production environment in parallel with the new end-user application environment.

Attaching the IT infrastructure development life cycle to the application development life cycle identifies the dependencies between organizations and resources. In addition, this process documents the information flow necessary to establish unified timelines for tasks and deliverables for project management. This ensures that the underlying IT services required by the end-user service level objectives are in place before end-users are introduced to the production environment.

Monitoring and Management

Service level management is the key to maintaining the production environment. By establishing the rules of engagement, the capabilities necessary to support the service level objectives, and the implementations of tools in the production environment, the entire production infrastructure can be monitored and measured. Violations of the scope defined in the SLAs and measured exceptions to the agreed-upon performance and management criteria can be addressed and resolved quickly, minimizing the impact on the business.

In this business reference model (see FIGURE 2-6), the flow of information is defined with the service desk established as the center of management information. The service desk controls information, brokers requests, audits request completion, and provides service level reporting services to the IT service management groups and business service end-user community.

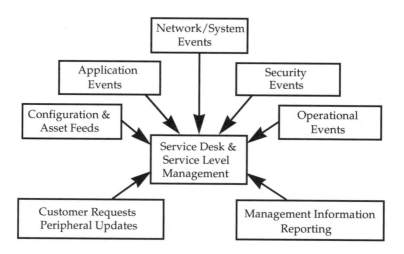

FIGURE 2-6   IT Business Reference Model - I

The service desk also brokers action items for the support organizations, both internal and external, and audits the completion, impact, and duration of service events (see FIGURE 2-7). With the dispatch of support activities controlled, the affected end-user service levels can be monitored. Monitoring end-user service levels enables vendor and end-user SLA and service level objective (SLO) adjustments, penalty assessment, enforcement, and arbitration where necessary.

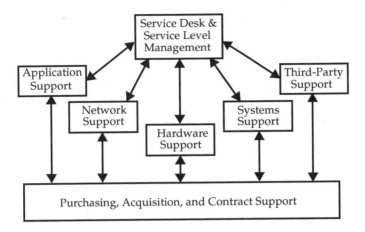

FIGURE 2-7 IT Business Reference Model - II

Measurement Principles

Assume that anything that is not measured is out of control.

- Measure the business as well as the computer systems and people.
- Measure and record trends in performance, cost, and availability.
- Measure things that you have no intention of tuning or controlling.

Although it may not be obvious, the mere act of measuring something is beneficial. There is a natural human instinct to observe measurements, and when a measure starts to behave in an odd way, it becomes noticeable and therefore can be corrected at an early stage.

You should not specify all the measurements in advance; however, it is beneficial to encourage end-to-end measurement as a culture among the staff. There are some stable and important measurement definitions imposed by management; but in addition, lightweight, evolving, ad hoc, and experimental measurements are extremely useful.

If the entire IT staff establishes how to measure everything that they do and decorates their walls with plots of those measurements, a large amount of corrective feedback will automatically blanket the systems and processes that run the business.

A system should be built to help the IT staff log arbitrary data into performance databases, both automatically and by hand. These databases should have summaries and graph plotting that anyone can use and should be as simple and lightweight as possible.

One important trade-off that must be made is deciding the priority of three conflicting ideals: fast, cheap, or safe. Make the decision with care to establish a balance. Parameterize each component separately and combine them into an availability hierarchy. Rate each component as %fast + %cheap + %safe = 100% to get relative proportions. Combine the components into a hierarchy so that high-level views are automatically given the combined priority. Combining reliability and availability metrics is well understood, but it is also important to at least estimate the relative cost and performance implications of the choices being made.

Conclusion

Production environment engineering and performance management may appear to be obscure forms of art. By studying the collective experiences of the traditional datacenter community and applying proven best practices through an organized and well-defined methodology of service coverage, the art can be converted into a well-understood science, with a predictable quality of results. Creating reusable templates, documents, and processes for design, implementation, and integration of datacenter services in production environments can result in higher quality of services, lower service delivery costs, and less replication of effort. Defining the framework, extended framework, reference models, and timelines and enforcing them within IT production environments can help deliver end-user services with repeatable quality of service. Defining these frameworks, models, and timelines determines what actions are necessary to keep the modern open-system datacenter as well-organized and well-managed as the best of the traditional mainframe predecessors.

The next chapter provides a methodology for service level management and looks at some problems of capacity estimation across multiple platforms.

CHAPTER 3

Suggested Processes

In medicine, prevention is almost always more efficient than cure, and it is a good idea to optimize your outlay on preventive medicine to help reduce the frequency and severity of illness. In the enterprise computing environment, you can accomplish a similar purpose by establishing, monitoring, and enforcing ongoing practices and processes.

Wherever possible, automate health monitoring and reporting for your systems. Automating the collection of data for the qualitative and quantitative properties of a measured service allows you to create baseline and trending information that is valuable to the capacity planning and load planning processes.

Development practices make a considerable difference, so we recommend that you include performance when determining internal application development guidelines. Measuring and reporting key performance criteria in an application development environment can help set release time expectations for performance and capacity. These practices can also help you recognize features and identify changes of performance implications of the application being developed. To establish the best internal application guidelines, it is important to:

- Define techniques and tools
- Use a common instrumentation and availability architecture
- Test and size applications before they reach production

These tools, their usage specifications, and the actions required at measured thresholds should be well-documented and placed in a system runbook. This runbook should provide the guidelines and standard process flows for reporting and acting on system events of many types. The system runbook should contain enough detail to reconstruct the procedures and operating environment in the production environment in the event of a disaster. This runbook should also be designed to enable an IT employee who is unfamiliar with the specific local environment to successfully implement the described procedures and threshold activities.

Create some breathing room for planning by defining a multilevel escalation path. Use a strict change control process, and schedule batches of changes to manage risk. Arrange for the appropriate staff to be on site during change periods, to concentrate on fire-fighting efforts. In a fast-changing business environment, the amount of change will keep increasing and this acceleration must be managed and controlled without impeding change.

This chapter highlights the importance of documenting service level agreements between service providers and users. Additionally, this chapter offers best practices for capacity estimation and consolidating workloads.

Service Level Management

Many client/server environments measure their service performance by CPU utilization, uptime/downtime, paging rates, I/O utilization, cache hit ratios, and the like. Though all of this is important, still more information is needed to understand the end-user's perspective. Users are more interested in the end-to-end availability of a service and the perceived notion of *slow* and *fast*. Unfortunately, these perceptions are difficult to quantify. The synthesis of traditional datacenter monitoring and the end-to-end availability of the service is required. This synthesis is known as service level management (SLM).

When IT departments first attempt to implement SLM, the tools are not always available. In such instances, it is appropriate to measure what *can* be measured. The goal is to eventually be able to measure from the end-user's service perspective. Once the new perspective of monitoring a service becomes more familiar to the IT department, the service level objectives (SLOs) can be expanded to include additional metrics from the end-user's perspective.

Service Level Agreements (SLAs)

Service level agreements are negotiated between consumers and providers of IT services. There could be multiple SLAs between a single business unit and multiple service providers, such as network, IT infrastructure, database, and desktop workstation support groups. Some providers can also have SLAs in place with other providers, including vendors and internal provider organizations whose services they consume. These multilevel SLA structures can help pass business requirements up, refining the requirements of the IT infrastructure. They can also pass capabilities down to the end-user level, providing technical capabilities in a business service context.

Most SLAs follow the same basic framework:

- A background is established for the service; it generally consists of what has been provided historically, the proposed service, and what the proposed service will provide:

- All parties are identified.
- The service is identified.
- Expected transaction load is projected.
- Metrics are established.
- Escalation procedures are clearly documented.
- Arbitration, costs, consequences, and terms are all clearly defined.

Keep in mind that one of the keys to a successful SLA is clear communication and realistic, measurable goals that are stated in terms of the consumer's needs.

The SLA should not be mired in legalese; rather, it should be easily understood by anyone who is familiar with the service and the specified area of business. The SLA should be implemented as part of the system runbook and maintained in an area accessible to both the business unit using the service and the IT staff maintaining the service.

The following list names the sections most commonly found in an SLA and describes what each should include:

- *Background* – Provide an overview of the SLA and historic information about the service that was previously provided. Additionally, general information about the SLA, the business processes and objectives, and the impact of the new SLA on the business processes should be included. This section should target readers who are unfamiliar with the service.

- *Parties* – Identify key contacts from all groups and the responsibilities of each. Clearly define the parties affected by this service. Who is the service provider and who is the consumer? Are there other affected groups, and whose expertise is needed?

- *Service definition* – Define the service being covered, location of the service (both the servers and the end-users), number of users, transaction volume expected, and service capacity. Determine coverage and schedules for the service, including service availability hours and maintenance windows. Be sure to include measurable goals for the service.

- *Key business indicators (KBIs)* – List in detail the number of concurrent users, transactions per unit of time (hours/minutes), transaction types, user distribution (LAN and WAN links and latency), resource contention with other applications, and workload intensities. This item should be very explicit.

- *Measurement of service* – Define the method by which the KBIs are measured, and track compliance with the service definition.

- *Problem reporting and escalation* – Establish the problem reporting process and escalation procedure.

- *Review and reporting* – Establish regular service reports and review meetings.

- *Costs, chargebacks, and consequences* – Establish costs for the service and chargeback processes. Define rewards or penalties for compliance/noncompliance.

- *Resolution of disputes and arbitration* – Define the arbitrators who will resolve disputes.
- *Reassessment and update of SLAs* – Establish a regular review cycle. Given the dynamic nature of IT environments (new applications, greater demand, or additional users), regular reviews are necessary to revise and update the SLAs.
- *Term* – Define valid dates of the SLA.
- *Approvals* – Acquire signoff of the SLA by heads of each party.
- *Definition of terms* – Provide a glossary of terms used in the SLA.

Each SLA should be unique, based on the service being provided and the needs of the users. However, this does not mean that once the first SLA has been completed it will be necessary to start again from scratch. There will be nuances for each service that is being placed in an SLA.

Identifying a Service

Given the user-centric focus of an SLA, the process of defining these agreements requires sales and marketing skills, tact and diplomacy, and the traditional IT abilities of managing and measuring IT resources.

When identifying a service for the initial implementation of an SLA, check that the existing service fits two criteria:

- Existing tools can monitor the service and the existing baseline data exists, including service availability and historic performance metrics.
- The dependencies for the service can be clearly defined and those groups that are required to provide components of the service are available (network, printing, help desk, etc.).

The implementation of an SLA is beneficial to both parties, providing resource consumption and service sizing information. An SLA can assist the IT department in projecting load planning information for system sizing, the business unit in estimating the cost of proposed changes to the service, and the accounting department in assigning real costing estimates for business services provided.

The Service Definition

Once a service has been defined, the technical components of that service need to be identified. Include the servers, networks, number of end-users, and their physical locations. Detail the projected transaction volume and service capacity for the systems, as well as the acceptable threshold. The goal is to include the lowest acceptable and desired average per transaction latency and maximum supported transaction rate for the service. List the core system availability hours and planned maintenance windows.

The *service definition* should be:

- Meaningful
- Measurable
- Understandable
- Cost-effective
- Attainable

Metrics for the service will be derived from meetings with the end-users, benchmarking, and historical data that includes uptime/downtime, outage times, and performance. All of these metrics should be mutually agreed upon by both the IT department and the users, and should represent explicit numbers with measurable goals. The SLA should be cost-effective for both the end-users and the IT department, while still meeting the demands of the business. Lastly, the goals should be attainable, based on testing and historic performance.

Example Service Definition:

The order processing group has 300 employees, all centrally located in the Kansas City facility. They are currently connecting to a database on a Sun Enterprise™ 6500 server, also located in the Kansas City facility, over the local area network (LAN). The order processing group must run monthly reports on the first week of every month (for the previous month), quarterly reports on the first week of every quarter (for the previous quarter), and annual reports on the first week of the new fiscal year (for the previous year).

Example Server Specification:

The server architecture for this environment consists of the following:

Sun Enterprise 6500 server

16 CPUs, 4 Gigabytes of memory

700-Gigabyte A3500

2 FDDI network adapters connected to the server LAN

Note that desktops, network infrastructure, help desk, backup, restore, and printer support are covered under a separate contract.

After characterizing the service and defining the infrastructure, establish the service time frames and windows of maintenance. Service specifications should be based on the needs of the users and the performance data acquired from previous years (if available).

Example Service Schedule Specification:

Business hours are defined as 0600 EST to 2000 EST, Monday through Sunday.

The maintenance windows are defined as 2030 EST until 0530 EST, Monday through Sunday. During these maintenance windows, no transactions are permitted.

If transactions are required during any of the maintenance windows, then prior approvals from the IT manager and the end-user manager are required. Approval must be secured and the request submitted to the help desk at least 7 days prior to the proposed request. At no time will transaction processing needs be allowed to compromise data or backup integrity.

In the event of an emergency, a planned outage may need to be scheduled outside the normal maintenance windows. In such a case, the IT department will seek the users' approval for the arrangement and timing of the outages. They will also make a reasonable attempt to limit the impact of the planned service outage to the end-users when possible.

In the event of a "disaster" requiring the recovery of data or the restoration of significant portions of the system, the help desk will notify the users of the service event and regular updates will be provided every 30 minutes until the service is restored. Those events defined as "disaster" will not be counted in the service availability calculations, but will be documented in the monthly service review.

Current estimations of disaster-level service restoration are two hours for system level restoration, four hours for application data recovery, and two hours for database system recovery. No system service event, including disaster events, shall exceed twelve hours.

Example Availability Specification:

Outages are periods during defined business hours that fall outside emergency maintenance windows and during which the system is unavailable for transactions. Planned or scheduled emergency maintenance is not included in outage calculations. Outage onset is the time that the outage is detected rather than the actual time of occurrence. Outage termination is the time that service is available after an outage.

The system shall maintain functional availability of 99.8% of business hours. System availability is determined by the following equation:

Coverage = Total minutes in month defined as "business hours"

14 hours per day × 60 minutes × 30 days = 25200 minutes

Outage = minutes of monthly outage (33 minutes)

Availability = (Coverage − Outage)/Coverage × 100

(25200 mins)–(33 mins) × 100 / (840 mins × 30 days) = 99.8%

During the peak hour, 95% of queries will be completed in less than 2 seconds (on average) with up to 300 users online. No queries will exceed 5 seconds.

During peak hour, 95% of all order transactions will be completed in less than 5 seconds (on average) with up to 300 users online. No queries will exceed 9 seconds.

The order processing system will sustain a transaction of 30,000 transactions per hour during business hours.

Because historical batch-related performance data is lacking, no guarantees of performance for batch processing can be made at this time.

Key Performance Indicators (KPIs)

KPI documents have long been the yardstick we have used to measure our server's performance. While SLAs are specified in business service terms, KPIs are defined in language familiar to the system administrator. They often measure available CPU, memory, and I/O throughput, as well as more granular aspects such as mutex counts, interrupts, and context switches. KPIs are not to be interpreted as pass/fail conditions, but are meant to report on the overall performance health of the server and to indicate when a service might not have adequate resources to meet the goals of the SLA.

After the service definition has been created, system performance goals are established to measure resource utilization against resource capacity. The KPI document establishes resource thresholds and identifies warning and critical levels of resource consumption.

When the capabilities of a service are being measured, a number of tests are performed on the server. Benchmarking of the application should be performed to identify the limits of the server's capabilities and to identify a baseline of the resources that the business service consumes at different thresholds of use.

TABLE 3-1 lists the kind of thresholds found in a KPI document.

TABLE 3-1 Key Performance Indicator Examples

Resource	Warning Threshold	Critical Threshold
CPU	>70% utilization for any measured shift	>90% utilization for any measured shift
Disk	>30% "%busy" for any measured shift	>50% "%busy" for any measured shift
Memory Scan Rate	>1000 pages per second, sustained for 5 minutes	>4000 pages per second, sustained for 5 minutes

The system architecture, both hardware and software, corresponds directly to the capacity and impact on the service. As the hardware architecture and software are changed by upgrades or patches, the KPI document should be revisited to determine new thresholds where necessary.

Most IT departments choose not to include KPIs in the actual SLA, because the details contained in the KPI document are intended for the IT department personnel directly involved in the management of the server system. These KPI measurements can be useful in budgeting, planning, and justifying upgrades and additional resources. They can also be used as the baseline to compare performance measurements against measurements made after modifications to the service applications, database, and desktop systems.

KPI Measurement

After identifying the KPIs, make sure that the measurement criteria and toolsets that monitor them are outlined in the KPI document.

A number of tools are available to help monitor system performance. Some of the tools including `sar`, `iostat`, `vmstat`, `mpstat`, and `netstat` are integrated into the Solaris OE to assist with KPI measurement. Free tools such as Sun™ Management Center (SunMC) and the SE-Toolkit provide graphical tools to monitor single systems. Commercial monitoring tools like SunMC, BMC Patrol, BMC Best/1, and TeamQuest can be configured to measure, monitor, and report on performance status and thresholds for a large number of systems. Most can then be integrated into enterprise management tools like Solstice Enterprise Manager™ software and HP's OpenView.

It may be necessary to create some of your own tools to monitor a service from the end-user's perspective. Although it is easy to monitor services from the back room, a regular snapshot of the user's response time is needed. Thus, network latency should be taken into account when possible. These custom tools need not be overly complex. In fact, a simple script that queries the server from the end-user's subnet and sends SNMP traps back to the network operation center (NOC) with response times may be sufficient.

TABLE 3-2 lists example tool definitions that correspond to the sample thresholds in TABLE 3-1.

TABLE 3-2 Tool Definitions for Key Performance Indicators

Resource	Tool	Sample Time
CPU	*sar* – utilization is determined by the sum of "%sys" and "%usr"	20 mins
Disk	*sar* – utilization is determined by "%busy"	20 mins
Memory (to Solaris 7 OE)	*vmstat* - scan rate as reported in the "*sr*" column	5 mins
Memory (from Solaris 8 OE)	*vmstat* - free memory as reported in the "*free*" column	5 mins

The example in TABLE 3-2 also illustrates a problem: Some metrics are vendor- or release-dependent, so multiple definitions need to be maintained.

When summarizing KPI data, keep in mind that there are different consumers of this data. First, there are the system administrators, who are usually adept at analyzing raw performance data. Next are the IT managers and financial planners, who need summaries of the data for budgeting. Last are the end-users, who may be interested in the system's health and performance. These last two groups may be best served by a Web page that provides graphical representations of system load and performance. Charts and graphs can better represent system health for less technical users. Chapter 6, "Observability," discusses audiences for performance information in more detail.

A KPI document can also include actions for immediate relief or resolution of performance events. These actions might include stopping, rescheduling, or reprioritizing running batch jobs, stopping other business functions that are deemed not to be business-critical, or running utilities for analyzing the current application load.

Problem Reporting and Escalation

To minimize impact and confusion for the users, use the existing problem-reporting process that is currently in place for that service (if the process exists and can be modified appropriately). This process should list the severity levels, the primary contacts at the help desk, and an escalation matrix for unresolved problems. Problem-reporting and escalation procedures should be well-documented in the system runbook. The procedures should be tested and updated as necessary to reflect changes to the IT environment.

Severity of problems can range anywhere from a single user having *slow* response to a global outage. To allocate resources appropriately, severity levels should be defined, as should the priority in which those levels are organized.

TABLE 3-3 lists a sample definition of severity levels.

TABLE 3-3 Sample Severity Levels

Level	Possible Impact
1 – Critical	Potential loss of customers Key business functions unavailable for one or more locations Major network outage More than 50% of workforce affected Possible revenue loss of >$100,000/hour Possible cumulative revenue loss of >$250,000 / hour
2 – High	Key business functions not working properly and is severely impacting one or more locations More than 25% of workforce affected Possible revenue loss of $50,000 – $100,000/hour Possible cumulative revenue loss of $50,000 – $250,000/hour
3 – Medium	A key business function experiencing problems and limiting the efficiency of a single group or location Loss of productivity for at least 25 people Possible revenue loss of between $20,000 – $50,000/hour
4 – Low	Fewer than 25 people affected Loss of productivity Possible revenue loss of <$20,000 Cumulative revenue loss of <$20,000
5 – Minor	Workforce experiencing a problem that is not affecting efficiency Workforce experiencing only minor loss of productivity No revenue or cost impact Customer request for information

A simple call sheet may suffice for the contact information. All calls, regardless of severity, should be placed through the main help desk for tracking and escalations.

During Critical- and High-level problems, the help desk should contact the next tier on the escalation list immediately in addition to the appropriate IT personnel responsible for resolution. The contact information for different components of the production environment should be documented in the system runbook, including how to contact the help desk itself, owners of different categories of problems, and vendors responsible for different components of the environment.

Delays in the resolution of a problem can also result in an escalation in severity level. Whether an automatic notification to the next support tier is made depends on the IT department's escalation method. The escalation path and events causing the escalation should be well-documented in the system runbook.

The following example is a guideline from a sample problem report sheet.

Sample Problem Report Sheet:

Problems should be reported to the IT help desk by phone to (606) 555-5300, by email to help@helpdesk, or by fax to (606) 555-5301. Faxed or emailed trouble reports will receive a call from a help desk engineer within 30 minutes of the receipt of the report during specified core business hours and within 2 hours outside of the specified core business hours.

Please provide the following information:
- *Name*
- *Department*
- *Location*
- *Phone*
- *Email*
- *Problem Description (including your desktop environment and application with which you are experiencing problems)*
- *Number of users affected*

The help desk will assign a severity level based on the problem description (and impact) and will contact the appropriate IT personnel.

If your problem is Level 1 (Critical) or Level 2 (High), the help desk will immediately notify the IT manager for that service and the appropriate IT engineers. The IT manager for the service will be notified of the problem every 60 minutes, until the problem is resolved.

Level 3 problems will be upgraded to Level 2 if not resolved in 3 business days.

Level 4 problems will be escalated to Level 3 if not resolved in 5 business days.

Trouble-Reporting Metrics

The service description should also include metrics relating to trouble reporting. These metrics should include the availability of the help desk, as measured by how long the customer should wait from the first ring when calling, and the effectiveness of the help desk, as defined by the percentage of calls answered while the customer is on the phone.

Reporting and Review

Regular reports should be made available to the end-users, business unit management, and IT management to indicate how well the IT department is doing with meeting the service description. Usually, these reports are weekly, with monthly, quarterly, and annual summaries. Reporting times will depend on the needs of the customer. The monthly, quarterly, and annual reports should also provide running averages of preceding months or quarters.

Regular reviews of the KPI documents and SLA should be performed. These reviews should be between the IT managers of the organization supporting the service and the end-user managers. The SLA is a tool for maintaining availability, so the importance of these meetings is paramount. In relatively static environments, quarterly meetings may be fine (with more frequent reports). However, within dynamic environments, such as growing e-commerce environments and service providers, these meetings should be performed monthly or weekly to determine any changes that need to be made to the service definition or the system and application infrastructure. In some extreme cases where changes to the planned load and service definition occur on a less predictable or projectable schedule, even a weekly service review may need to be complemented with impromptu meetings to provide maximum advance notice of change to the parties providing the service.

At these meetings, discuss the performance of the IT department in meeting the service description goals, the new requirements, and growth expectations of the end user. Identify problems that arose during the previous week and possible recommendations for ways to improve those problems. This is also a good time to clarify any questions about the agreement. It is much better to resolve questions early on in the life of the SLA, rather than later through arbitration.

A sample weekly report is described in "Management Viewpoint Implementation" on page 135.

Costs, Chargebacks, and Consequences

One of the key benefits of creating SLAs is that they enable organizations to predict the resources required to support a service. Though it is always a painful process to comb through historical performance and trouble ticket data, the reward is the ability to predict the actual costs incurred to support a service more accurately.

Future service requirements exposed as a result of these meetings may affect personnel resources and computing resources, thereby justifying additional people or hardware.

In the original example, it was determined that the resources listed in TABLE 3-4 were needed to support the order processing group for the first year.

TABLE 3-4   Example Support Costs

Staff Headcount	Fractional Headcount Required	Salary*	Total*
Help Desk Staff 1	1.00	$45,000	$45,000
Help Desk Staff 2	0.50	$45,000	$22,500
UNIX Admin	0.45	$80,000	$36,000
DBA	0.25	$80,000	$20,000
Operator	0.50	$50,000	$25,000
Network Admin	0.25	$80,000	$20,000
Manager	0.25	$100,000	$25,000
TOTAL		$480,000	$193,500

*Note that these numbers do not include taxes, benefits, additional training, etc.

For the end-user department to hire the talent needed, the department would need to spend approximately $480,000 a year. Moreover, these resources would be dedicated to that department, have no support structure (other IT department mentors), and considerable idle time (unless there were lots of problems with the service).

By maintaining support for the service in a centralized IT department, the end-user business unit can attain coverage by the IT department at nearly 40% of the original costs ($193,500 ÷ 480,000) × 100). This savings is enhanced by the following benefits:

- IT staff are not necessarily dedicated to a single service; their time is often shared among multiple services.

- Mentoring from other IT department engineers provides cross-training and skill enhancement throughout the support staff.

- The datacenter environment, rather than the standalone environment, provides higher quality, sharable, standardized resources for backup, restoration, monitoring, management, and reporting.

- The IT department can provide career paths and training, so key talent won't be as likely to leave.

- The engineers can standardize on datacenter disciplines, resulting in a move from reactive to more proactive management practices.

By identifying the projects on which engineers are spending the most time, the IT manager can identify recurring problems, find ways to rectify those problems, and lower the time spent by engineers. This increases the ability of the IT staff to address problem resolution. It also increases the leverage that the support organizations can wield over vendors, while lowering direct costs such as tool licensing and support contract costs.

Finally, there are the consequences of meeting or failing the service definitions. In some IT departments, the IT department staff's bonuses are directly tied to meeting or exceeding stated service level goals. In other environments, failure to meet stated service goals results in discounted or free services to the end-users. The consequences or rewards depend on your corporate support and culture.

An example of free service due to outage is as follows:

eBay:[1]

"For any hard outage lasting two or more hours, eBay will automatically extend listings for 24 hours and automatically credit all associated fees for affected listings. The following listings will be eligible for extension and credit:

"Any listing scheduled to end during the hard outage

"Any listing scheduled to end in the hour after the end of the hard outage"

Arbitration and Conflict Resolution

Even with regular meetings and clear lines of communication, problems can arise. These issues can be the result of misinterpretation of the service definitions, failure to meet proposed definitions, or just a breakdown in communication between the IT department and the end-users. During these times, it may be necessary to seek arbitration for a resolution.

Arbitration need not be an outside organization, though it very well can be. It can be a person or a panel that can review the problems and reach a final, binding solution. Since the point of arbitration is resolution, the decision of the arbitration panel is final.

Quite often, the arbitration panel will consist of the vice president of the IT department, the vice president of the end-user department, and one other person outside of the two organizations (maybe a CFO, HR director, or another vice president).

When creating the SLA, identify the members of the arbitration panel and gain their commitment from the onset. Once this approval is granted, the panel should be clearly identified in the SLA and its decisions adhered to by all involved.

---

1. From eBay, Inc.'s "Outage Policy," http://pages.ebay.com/help/community/png-extn.html, February 26, 2000.

Reassessment and Updating

The managers and representatives of the service for both the IT department and the end-users should meet regularly to review the existing SLA and to propose changes to the agreement. Either party may propose changes, but both parties must approve the changes.

Generally, changes are requested when there are significant deviations from the original service objectives, actual or expected changes to the IT environment, or new business requirements.

Regularly scheduled inspections of the agreement should also be held, and plans for end-user or IT department growth should be discussed at this time (if they have not already been addressed and resolved in previous meetings). Since SLAs are expected to be ongoing and of indefinite duration, these meetings provide a good time to review the previous period's performance and to suggest changes for the upcoming period. The time periods and review schedules should be documented in the system runbook. The system runbook should also contain the point of contact in one of the involved organizations responsible for scheduling the meeting and contacting the necessary parties for attendance.

Inventorying the Enterprise

Before you can project system requirements or specify hardware platforms, you must first know what the enterprise actually contains. A baseline must be created, containing the current processing capacity and computing resources consumed. In addition, this baseline must include overall hardware infrastructure and the total costs incurred by the enterprise in supporting computing needs.

Tools such as Gartner Group's TCO tool can provide estimated and true cost analysis of a computing infrastructure. Total costs must include:

- Real estate
- Server and infrastructure assets
- Depreciation
- Lease and rental fees
- Support
- Maintenance
- Professional services
- Education
- Training
- Software costs

A complete TCO analysis is a long and involved process, but can be very enlightening; such an analysis can reveal hidden and forgotten costs in the IT budget.

The computing needs for the business function must also be quantified in some manner. This quantification can resolve to individual business functions such as *payroll* and *marketing data* or can be further subdivided into more specific metrics such as *paychecks processed* or *trade show leads generated*.

Once the computing needs for the business function have been identified, the computing resources dedicated to those business functions should be inventoried. Databases, server software, server platforms, application software, and client-side desktops should be categorized and summarized by business function and computing category. In some cases, especially in the case of desktop computer platforms, resources will be shared among several unrelated business functions. These shared resources should be inventoried and characterized for an estimated percentage of use in each identified business function for which they are used.

Some *business functions* are not so easily identified and are often overlooked. These commonly include system and network management resources, as well as development, test, and prototyping environments, which may be very dynamic in configuration and structure.

All of these factors can be tallied against each other to define the current cost and performance characteristics of the business and computing environment. Results such as *server, maintenance*, and *support costs of the payroll system* can be generated from the collected data for comparisons and projections against the business growth potential and relative cost analysis of changes to the server platform or architecture.

Baselining Business Services

Baselining the performance of business services is the second step in understanding exactly what is happening in the datacenter. Performance baselines should measure each business function in terms of transaction type, transactional volume, and where possible, average response times for the driving server systems, in both *average* and *peak* transactional periods.

As an example of a performance baseline summary statement, an analysis of an online sales and distribution system might state that:

> Shift average transactional volumes for the sample period of 10/1/99 through 12/31/99 were measured as 12,000 catalog system lookups per hour. For shift hours measured at 11,500 to 12,500 transactions per hour, catalog system lookup response time averaged 3.2 seconds, with a worst-case query response time of 5.1 seconds.

A peak hourly rate of 22,000 catalog system lookups was measured for the hour of 19:00 PST on 12/23/99. During this peak-measured hour, catalog system lookup response time averaged 4.4 seconds, with a worst-case query response time of 11.4 seconds.

By measuring current business functions over a representative period of business traffic, we can establish quantitative as well as qualitative metrics. We can then use the collected metrics to project future requirements and system capabilities, and to set user and management expectations for service qualities relative to service volumes.

By creating a scalar representation of the performance characteristics of a particular business service, we accomplish two goals:

- Being able to predict application impacts of service load to help application developers and database administrators identify bottlenecks and inefficiencies in server and application software

- Plotting the linear scalability (or lack thereof) of a particular service to help predict the future resource needs for business function growth[1]

Capacity Estimation and Consolidation Processes

This section describes these processes in general, and Chapter 5, "Capacity Estimation," presents a detailed example of the implementation of these processes.

Quantifying Capacity

One of the most difficult tasks in workload performance analysis and characterization is predicting the quantity of work that disparate server platforms can support. This challenge is slightly easier when the servers being compared are of the same base architecture (UltraSPARC™) or, at the very least, from the same vendor (Sun Microsystems).

If there is an industry-standard benchmark that closely imitates your workload characteristics, then use that benchmark as a guideline for platform comparisons. Unfortunately, very few business implementations come at all close to the popular industry-standard benchmarks; or more appropriately stated, very few industry benchmark standards have any real meaning in actual business application computing.

1. The prediction is accomplished through the application of Amdahl's Law for parallel scalability of software systems.

Several commercial packages for performance monitoring and capacity planning include relative performance metrics for a variety of hardware and operating system environments. Two examples that we can use as samples of market offerings are BMC (formerly BGS) Best/1 and TeamQuest. The Best/1 and TeamQuest performance monitoring capabilities implement slightly different methods for capacity metrics, but both packages supply the same basic function.

Best/1 Performance Console for UNIX has an internal database of hardware and operating capabilities and assigns relative metrics to the processing and I/O capabilities of a given platform. Performance of a given system is quantified and can be used as input into the BEST/1 modeller for system sizing.

TeamQuest uses an external table to assign relative system capacity metrics. System performance can be recorded and applied against a chosen platform's capacity. This manual process can be a bit cumbersome in a large enterprise datacenter, but it allows the user to create or expand on the default capabilities datasets provided in the product.

Consolidating Workloads

The actual process of consolidating workloads is fairly straightforward, once the workload baseline has been established. To combine workloads in a single-server platform, the workload baseline metrics are summed and the supporting hardware is sized to meet the projected computing needs. Target system peak shift and peak hours are chosen for sizing, and target system utilization is established for those time periods. Without strict resource management implementations, the rule of thumb for target utilization is 70%. With resource management software and policies implemented, target utilizations of 90% or more can be safely projected.

If the measured workloads exhibit unpredictable behavior (such as intermittent spikes in resource utilization or noncyclic resource consumption trends), the target utilization point might be lowered to accommodate the *worst-case* periods of consumption. The analysis of workload performance metrics, combined with a formal SLA, describe the transactional and service level expectations for the business computing function.

Directly relating business and service goals to server sizing and management considerations is a key byproduct benefit of a server consolidation project. Business projections for growth and service level expectations can be associated with system platform hardware, software, and licensing requirements for budgeting and IT resource planning of the project life cycle.

Resource Management

When multiple business functions are run within a single-server platform, resource conflicts almost always surface. Some applications will parallelize very well, running their workload more efficiently at the expense of the other workloads on the shared platform. To reduce the impact of these resource conflicts, formal resource management policies must be established and enforced according to SLA guidelines.

The Sun Enterprise 10000 platform supports dynamic system domains (DSDs), allowing a single-server platform to act as several distinct servers, with independent instances of the operating system and independent application environments. System resources can be migrated manually between system domains, allowing administrators to reallocate idle resources from an underused domain to a domain starving for resources. Resources can only be migrated at a system board level; in addition, no automated or performance policy-based dynamic reconfiguration (DR) is supported at this time.

Solaris OE processor sets allow the administrator to bind applications to a set of defined processors. Processor sets create hard walls of CPU resource allotment for each designated workload. Idle CPU resources within a processor set cannot be used by other workloads outside that processor set; in addition, idle CPU resources outside a processor set cannot be used by a workload starving within its processor set. The allocated CPU resources defined by processor sets can be dynamically adjusted; however, no automated process exists for policy-based CPU resource management.

Solaris Resource Manager (SRM) provides a policy-based resource framework for server resources that overcomes some of the limitations of processor sets and system domains. SRM is a *fair share* resource-scheduling system, capable of managing resource categories such as CPU, virtual memory, connect time, logons, and disk quotas.

Resources are defined as either *static* or *renewable*, depending on their particular characteristics. A CPU is one example of a renewable resource because CPU resources are dynamic for any given point in time. There is no finite limit of CPU power; as a machine runs, new processing power is always available. Static resources include items like *number of simultaneous logons permitted* and *connect time per session*.

With SRM, renewable resources that a workload does not consume within its *share* boundaries are free for use by other workloads. Resource consumption is governed by the relative shares allocated to the cohabiting workloads. Workloads can consume any idle renewable resources on demand. When renewable resources are not available, SRM will enforce throttles against any process currently consuming more than its defined relative shares.

Resource management can include combinations of SRM, processor sets, and dynamic system domains. These tools can complement each other, and they offer excellent provisions for resource management architecture. In addition, these tools can safely control resource utilization within the guidelines of the SLA and KPI documents. Refer to the Sun BluePrints book *Resource Management* for more detailed information on SRM.

The Never-Ending Cycle

Like system and network management, performance and workload management define a never-ending cycle. System platforms, operating systems, application software, and the business functions that use them are in a continuous evolutionary progression. To properly consolidate server functions and satisfy business requirements, a complete understanding of the enterprise is necessary. This understanding must range from the business view of a service to the hardware impact of a running application.

When a successful implementation of a business-computing component is complete it is time for celebration. However, the celebration is short-lived because the close of one system implementation signifies the start of ongoing management of the underlying architecture. A well-monitored and managed computing environment will directly influence the modelling and prediction of the next incarnation of the architecture evolution. In addition, this environment will ensure that the computing resources provided for the business application will meet the requirements necessary to honor the contracted service levels.

When service levels exceed the limits defined or key performance indicators exceed defined limits, the platform must be reviewed and possibly upgraded to meet the defined business goals. In addition, the platform may need to have workloads balanced in the computing enterprise to allocate more resources to the underperforming workload.

Even the hardware and software procurement process is circular. Business groups contract service levels with capacity planners. Capacity planners define a workload metric for the service levels contracted. Systems engineers specify a hardware platform that can satisfy the workload metric and place a procurement request for the business group to budget.

Summary

This chapter highlighted the significance of establishing effective service level management and also demonstrated the importance of defining and maintaining a service level agreement between service providers and users. In addition, best practices were offered for inventorying the enterprise and establishing a baseline for business services. Finally, this chapter suggested processes for quantifying capacity and consolidating workloads and described the impact of capacity estimation using industry benchmarks across multiple platforms.

The next chapter provides a recipe for successful scenario planning and presents a methodology for modelling capacity and load.

Scenario Planning

Using management inputs and modelling alternative scenarios, you can predict the effects of workload mix changes, marketing-driven load changes, performance tuning, and hardware upgrades. Start by determining trends of recent history, then add forward prediction using business inputs to predict what the future workload should look like.

Trending techniques use a mixture of step functions that track changes in your configuration and a technique sometimes known as multivariate adaptive statistical filtering (MASF). This process extracts cyclic variations from your data so that you can see the underlying trends. With this technique, you use analytical models to predict the behavior of complex workloads that consist of several classes of user and transaction types.

You should not attempt to build a detailed model of every part of your system. Such models are too complex, too hard to calibrate, and would never be finished in time to be useful. Model the primary workloads; make sure you include the ones like order entry, which make money for your business.

This chapter provides a guide to successful scenario planning and provides best practices for using spreadsheets to create a model for capacity and load. In addition, this chapter presents methods for tweaking the model to enhance accuracy.

A Recipe for Successful Scenario Planning

Successful planning must be based on firm foundations. It is quite common for planning to be attempted and then abandoned as a technique because the effort put in was misdirected and the return on investment (i.e., useful planning results obtained) was too low. This recipe provides a step-by-step guide to the process and gives examples of the kind of information that needs to be recorded in each step.

1. Sketch a simplified system architecture.

You probably have an overall system diagram showing every machine, every network, and all kinds of other details. You need to reduce the complexity by looking for the primary flows through the system. These are usually the flows that either are subject to SLAs or are money-makers for the business. The initial sketch should be based on the physical systems in place, since that is the simplest place to start. When multiple systems are employed to do the same job, show them as a simple replicated set, even if they are not exactly the same. Be ruthless about paring down the complexity to a minimum to start with. It is better to go too far in this direction and add systems back in later than to start off with a too-complex architecture and get bogged down trying to model it. FIGURE 4-1 shows an example of a physical architecture sketch.

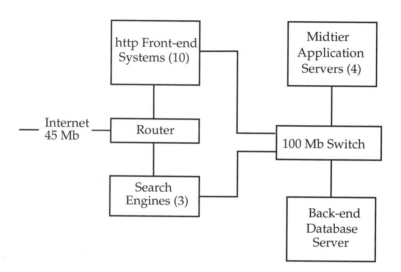

FIGURE 4-1   Example Physical Architecture Sketch

The physical sketch usually needs to be supplemented by a dataflow sketch (FIGURE 4-2) that shows the way the main classes of users and applications are connected.

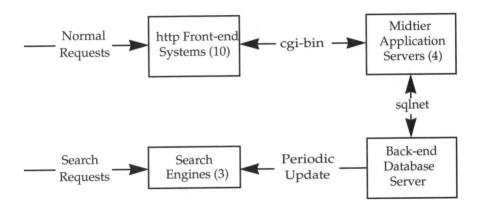

FIGURE 4-2 Example Dataflow Architecture Sketch

These sketches provide a framework to which information can be attached. Later steps in this recipe refer to the systems and flows.

2. **Determine primary bottlenecks.**

The model should concentrate on the primary bottlenecks. It may be sufficient to look at just the CPU load on a central database server, or you may also need to watch network capacity or a wider range of systems, depending on your situation. The bottlenecks will change over time, so they must be listed explicitly each time a scenario is modelled.

For each of the systems and network interfaces that are identified in the physical sketch, record an average utilization during the peak usage period. Record the utilization of each network interface as a percentage. For shared network components, measure the combined utilization of the network backbone or switch. For each system, you need to know the overall CPU utilization and the utilization of the busiest disk on that system. The highest utilizations you find are the components most likely to be the primary bottlenecks. FIGURE 4-3 shows an example of a physical architecture sketch with utilizations.

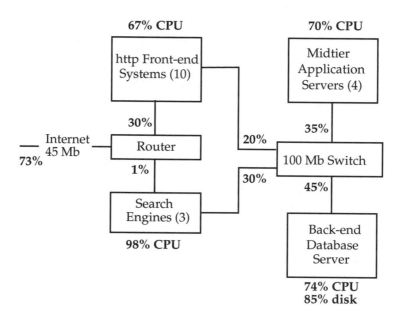

FIGURE 4-3 Example Physical Architecture Sketch With Utilizations

The example shown in FIGURE 4-3 illustrates a system where the primary bottlenecks appear to be the CPU and disk on the back-end database and the CPU on the search engines. Disk utilizations were found to be very low on the other systems, which operate mainly from memory caches.

3. **Measure service levels and workload intensities.**

   If you have an SLA or some estimates for response times and throughput, then annotate the data flow architecture sketch with both the latencies and frequency of transactions wherever this can be determined or estimated (see FIGURE 4-4).

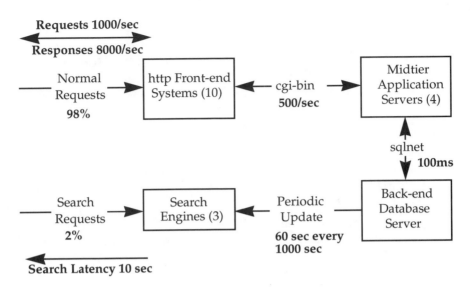

FIGURE 4-4 Dataflow Architecture With Latencies and Intensities

4. **Determine operational modes.**

Performance modelling assumes that the workload is essentially constant. Therefore, if the system has periodic changes in behavior, it is best to pick out the main modes and measure and model them separately. One of the main modes occurs when backups are taking place. In many cases, backups must take place online during quiet periods, because when you are supporting Internet-based users around the world, there is no convenient time for offline backups. Modelling backup behavior is useful, as fast-growing environments will find that the amount of data to back up increases rapidly. As a result, the backup duration increases and often overspills from the quiet period, affecting performance. The disk subsystem will probably be at its busiest during backup.

In the example shown in the figures, there is a periodic search update, and the load is different while the update is occurring. It is useful to model behavior in the normal state and also during an update. It seems possible that the back-end server's network interface would be a bottleneck during the update. The utilization levels are different in each mode, so they need to be recorded separately.

5. Choose one bottleneck.

It is quite simple to model a single function on a single system, and extremely complicated to model an entire network of systems. However, the performance of a network of systems is limited by its bottleneck, so you get useful results simply and quickly by focusing on one core bottleneck and assuming that bottlenecks elsewhere in the system can be removed fairly easily.

One way of looking at this issue is that the biggest and most expensive system you have should be run at the highest utilization, so that you are not wasting an expensive resource by leaving it idle. This system then tends to be the bottleneck and is the best candidate for modelling. You should find it more cost-effective to upgrade surrounding systems so that they are no longer bottlenecks.

In the example, the back-end database server is a single system (or perhaps a highly available pair of systems); it is common for this system to be both the most expensive resource and also the primary bottleneck. It is much easier to replicate smaller systems to take care of front-end services than to decompose a single database instance into multiple systems.

6. Choose service and utilization indicators.

The initial model should be a crude and oversimplified base for planning future scenarios. The hardest thing to learn for successful modelling is to let go of the details. You can build a very useful model with incomplete and inaccurate data as long as you are smart in what you include and what you leave out. For the back-end server, a mixture of transactions is taken from the application servers. However, as long as that mixture remains fairly constant, you can average all transactions into a generic transaction rate. If the back-end server load level fluctuates a lot because of several competing applications, you need to perform a workload breakdown to obtain just the CPU and disk utilization that is involved in servicing the incoming transactions. If this is the primary load on the system, then you can probably get away with using the overall CPU utilization. Assume that there is a direct linear relationship between the total number of transactions processed and the CPU utilization. The average CPU time per transaction may change when the system configuration or application changes. However, the characteristics of the system remain constant between changes and provide a useful basis for a simple growth model.

7. Pick a large time scale.

For scenario planning, we are interested in what will happen over the coming days, months, and years, not the next few seconds—this is why we can ignore so much fine detail. Also, to quote the mainframe capacity-planning guru Pat Artis:

> To predict the future, you must know the past.

You need to collect historical data that spans a time period similar to the period you are trying to predict. So, a week's collected data gives you a good prediction of next week. To predict the next year, you need collected data for the whole of the previous year. If you want to separate time-based or seasonal variations from one-off events, you need to see the same season twice. Lack of data is no excuse; however, you should start to plan immediately and as time goes by, the extra historical data will improve the quality of your predictions.

8. **Work through the planning process.**

   The rest of the scenario modelling and planning process is illustrated with a simple parameterized spreadsheet in the next section.

9. **Compare the prediction with reality.**

   Once you have predicted the transaction rate and system utilization for the coming months, you need to measure and compare with reality. This way, you learn which estimates in the model were optimistic or pessimistic and how to build better models.

10. **Recalculate the predictions regularly.**

    After each time period you predict (e.g., monthly), you have a new baseline of real data and you must recalculate the model needs.

In the next section, a simple spreadsheet-based scenario planning model is explained. It should be quick and easy to implement, and if nothing else, it should help you think more clearly about the assumptions you are making over the coming months and years.

Modelling Capacity and Load

This section explains how a spreadsheet can be used to quickly generate estimates of capacity and load. By combining projected effects of various influences on load at any given time (such as growth of the user base and seasonal variation), you can generate a model that projects the total future load on the system. A model that considers the current capacity a baseline and then estimates performance improvements from various effects can be used in conjunction with the load model to determine if the system will have the capacity to support the required load in the future.

Modelling Load

Several influences on load are introduced in the subsequent sections. For each such influence, a mathematical model appropriate for predicting future behavior is presented. These models will be appropriate in a wide variety of circumstances, but they can also be easily modified to better model a specific environment. For each of the influences presented, the formulas presented in the descriptions can be used to create a spreadsheet that estimates the "growth factor" from a baseline. If additional influences have an impact on the load, they can be computed in a manner similar to the influences described below and can be combined with the other influences to get a total load. Additionally, different models can be used for the influences described below if the models provided aren't sufficient.

The basic idea of the spreadsheet modelling aid presented here is that the effect of any influence at a given time can be represented as an independent growth factor that represents how that influence affects the load. The growth factor is simply the factor that the original (baseline) load must be multiplied by to get the estimated load supported at the time in question. If the baseline load was measured in January and the estimated growth factor for June is 2.0, this means that the load can be expected to increase two-fold from January to June.

Because the growth factors are represented as multipliers, the units are immaterial. Load is plotted, but all the values are normalized. This means that they are divided by a normalization value. For repetitive influences like daily, weekly, or seasonal variation, the normalization value is the highest value present. For absolute (nonrepetitive) influences, the normalization value is the original (baseline) load. In either case, all the values are divided by the normalization factor to obtain the growth factors. When this occurs, the units of measurement cancel each other out. However, to obtain meaningful results, the same units should be used for all measurements. The units in a particular installation should be a meaningful measurement that represents the bottleneck—for instance: transactions per second, reads per second, network throughput, or CPU usage. In the example below, the measurements are of CPU load, because the CPU is the bottleneck. Determining the appropriate bottleneck is described in "A Recipe for Successful Scenario Planning" on page 47. The spreadsheet method outlined here is designed for systems with only one significant bottleneck. Systems with multiple bottlenecks need to use more complex methods.

Once all influences are computed in a spreadsheet, you can combine them by multiplying the growth factors for each influence together. An example of this is shown in TABLE 4-1 and in FIGURE 4-5.

It is also important to do a sanity check of the models. For instance, even if capacity planning shows a growth rate of 2 times month over month for several months while data is being gathered, projecting the trend may not be appropriate. Projecting this trend would lead to an estimate of load at the end of the year being 4096 times the baseline. Because many unmeasurable factors affect growth, this approach may not be appropriate. However, the spreadsheet model is flexible enough to allow for tailoring the models. More complex formulas can be used, or different formulas can be used for different time spans. For instance, the assumption could be made that the geometric exponential growth rate tapers off after a few months as a higher percentage of the limited target population becomes users. This could be implemented in the spreadsheet by using a growth factor of 2 for the first 4 months, followed by 1.5 for the subsequent months. Modifying the spreadsheet so that it better estimates the load and capacity of the systems in question is discussed in "Tweaking the Model" on page 74.

A final important consideration is that the time scales of each spreadsheet must coincide. For instance, if one spreadsheet measures growth as the result of a marketing campaign on a day-by-day basis and another spreadsheet measures growth as a result of seasonal effects on a monthly basis, they cannot be combined. The number of data points (spreadsheet cells) should also be the same for each influence. Additionally, it is important that the seasonal variations begin with the baseline in the correct season. For instance, if the baseline was taken in April, it is important that the seasonal cycle in the spreadsheet starts in April.

Daily and Weekly Variations

Note – Although daily and weekly variations are discussed below, they are not actually used in the example because other influences in the example are measured month-by-month.

The chart in FIGURE 4-5 shows most of a week from Tuesday to Sunday on a busy back-end server system in terms of transactions per second. Each transaction queries or updates the database and is a good indicator of the business activity level for this system. You can see that the system never sleeps, but there is a predictable pattern that peaks in the evening during weekdays and falls off a little during the weekend.

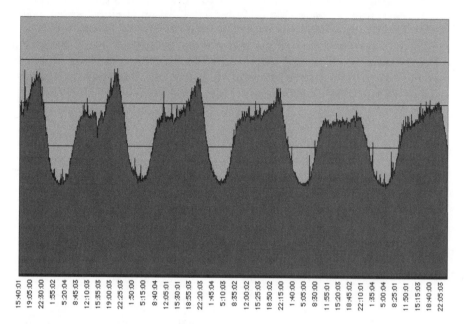

FIGURE 4-5 Daily Workload Variations Example

The important data is the *prime time* daily peak level. If the prime time is plotted day after day, then a pattern like the factors shown in TABLE 4-1 will emerge.

From the detailed information shown in FIGURE 4-5, all you really need is the typical daily peak level. The peak is most important, because good performance during peak loads is required to keep the users happy and make them more likely to visit the site in the future. The actual data from several weeks can be analyzed to extract the typical day-to-day variation or enable it to be estimated.

TABLE 4-1 is part of the spreadsheet; you enter your own score levels in the rightmost column to rate each day. These scores are normalized by the busiest day (in this case, Monday or Tuesday). This data is then charted so you can see the daily variation repeated for four weeks.

TABLE 4-1   CPU Peak Load Factor by Weekday

Day	Normalized Peak Load (Peak Load Divided by Max Peak Load)	Peak Load
Sunday	0.64	0.70
Monday	1.00	1.10
Tuesday	1.00	1.10
Wednesday	0.91	1.00
Thursday	0.91	1.00
Friday	0.91	1.00
Saturday	0.55	0.60

The chart in FIGURE 4-6 shows the peak level day by day. In this case, Monday is shown as the busiest day, with Friday a little lower, and a quieter weekend. Sundays are often busier than Saturdays, partly because systems located in California are near the end of the international dateline; hence, when it is Sunday in California, it is already Monday in the Asia-Pacific region.

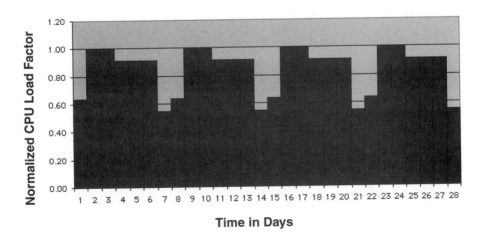

FIGURE 4-6   Chart of Daily Workload Variation Factor

There are three ways to obtain the weekday variation coefficients. The first way is to simply guess at something that "looks about right." Guesses are better if they are made by consensus with a group of people. The second way is to take measured data for several weeks, average all the data in a spreadsheet, and measure the daily peaks. The third way is to use statistical analysis, specifically analysis of variance (usually known as ANOVA), to fit a model to the data. This technique is described in a paper by Joe Hellerstein et al., published at the 1998 Computer Measurement Group conference. The paper uses several months' worth of Web site hit rate data collected in 1996 on www.sun.com by Adrian Cockcroft as its raw measurements, and fits an increasingly sophisticated model to the daily, weekly, and monthly variations.

Seasonal Effects

In addition to the variations from day to day, there are seasonal effects from month to month throughout the year. In the rest of this scenario planning exercise, monthly data is the basis of the plan. Within each month there will be daily variations, but the time scale over which changes and upgrades can be made to a production system is measured in months. Therefore, the peak load needs to be sustainable in any given month.

If you have at least a years' worth of collected data, you can use it to generate your estimates for the monthly variations. Keep in mind that if you have limited historical data, it is likely that the perceived seasonal effects will be a combination of the actual seasonal effect and other (potentially large) influences such as geometric exponential growth. "Tweaking the Model" on page 74 offers guidelines on how to make the model fit the data by use of a simple iterative tweaking method.

Alternatively, you should come up with estimates by consensus with your colleagues. You can enter these estimates into the spreadsheet as scores in the form shown in TABLE 4-2. As before, the scores are normalized to a maximum of 1.0.

TABLE 4-2 Seasonal Load Variations by Month

Month	Normalized Monthly Peak Load (Monthly Peak Load Divided by Max Peak Load)	Peak Load
January	0.89	8.0
February	0.72	6.5
March	0.61	5.5
April	0.56	5.0
May	0.44	4.0
June	0.39	3.5
July	0.33	3.0
August	0.33	3.0
September	0.78	7.0
October	0.89	8.0
November	1.00	9.0
December	1.00	9.0

FIGURE 4-7 shows a graph of seasonal load variations by month.

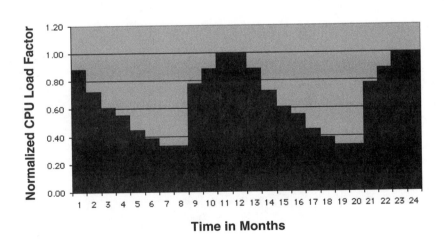

Time in Months

FIGURE 4-7 Chart of Seasonal Load Variations by Month

Two years of example data are shown in FIGURE 4-7, starting with January. This pattern depends on external events as well as the nature of the business. It must be determined and calibrated against business metrics, but other factors must first be taken into account. This is shown in the next few charts, which together will form a month-by-month predicted load level.

Geometric Exponential Growth

The growth of the Internet combined with a growth in awareness of your site may cause a geometric exponential growth in load levels. This can be easily expressed in two numbers as a growth factor over a time period. For example, growth might be expressed as 50% per quarter, or doubling in a year.

Note – The type of growth described here is mathematically referred to as geometric growth. However, because it is usually (somewhat incorrectly) referred to as exponential growth, it is referred to as geometric exponential growth here to avoid confusion.

A spreadsheet computes the growth factor and monthly factors for the coming months with a growth rate and duration provided by a user. The computation is based on the following formula:

$$L_t = L_0(G + 1)^{t-t_0}$$

In this case, t is the time (in whatever units you are using); L_t is the load at time t; L_0 is the baseline load value at time t_0; and G is the growth per time unit. If capacity planners have measured the growth over a given time period (and can safely assume the growth is geometric), they can extrapolate the growth rate (G) at a given time.

For instance, TABLE 4-3 shows a month-by-month growth that extrapolates from a growth of 1.5 times in 3 months. Using the known growth of 1.5 times in 3 months, the G can be solved for and substituted into the original formula. Since, the values for G and L_0 are known and can be substituted into the formula, the load at a given time (L_t) is computed based only on the time ($t - t_0$). The value t_0 is zero if t is measured in relation to it. In the following table, the values used are $G = .22$ and $L_0 = 1$, which makes the following formula:

$$L_t = 1.14^t$$

This formula is provided in a capacity planning spreadsheet to generate the values presented in the following sections. This spreadsheet is available at http://www.sun.com/blueprints/tools and has all of the appropriate formulas in place—you only have to enter the growth over a given period.

TABLE 4-3 shows an example of geometric exponential growth in user activity.

TABLE 4-3 Geometric Exponential Growth in User Activity

Month	Growth Factor
0	1
1	1.1
2	1.3
3	1.5
4	1.7
5	2.0
6	2.3
7	2.6
8	2.9
9	3.4
10	3.9
11	4.4
12	5.1
13	5.8
14	6.6
15	7.6
16	8.7
17	10.0
18	11.4
19	13.0
20	14.9
21	17.1
22	19.6
23	22.4
24	25.6

When plotted, the growth rate in TABLE 4-3 looks like the graph shown in FIGURE 4-8

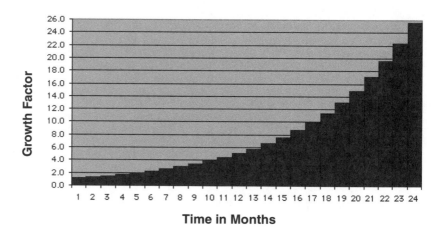

FIGURE 4-8 Chart of Geometric Exponential Growth Rate

There is an underlying growth factor involved in the size of the total Internet marketplace. At one point this was doubling about every 100 days, but recent growth rates suggest a doubling period of a year or more. The average activity level of Internet users also changes over time, increasing with the roll-out of broadband DSL and cable connections. Several large Internet sites are seeing business grow at a rate of about 50% every three months, or a doubling period of just under six months. This translates into the geometric exponential growth shown in FIGURE 4-8. After two years, the monthly load level is about 25 times higher than at the start. Your growth rate will vary and may not continue at this rate for this long, but some kind of growth model needs to be estimated and then calibrated against experience over time. For systems in which growth is not a geometric exponential, other formulas can be used to describe growth more closely.

Note that you should tune the growth rate as you obtain more data. Computing the growth rate over several different time ranges (for instance, January to March, March to May, and May to July) and averaging the results may yield a much better estimate of the growth. Also, continually estimating the growth rate will tell you if the geometric exponential growth rate is speeding up or slowing down, either of which could limit the effectiveness of the model.

Marketing Events

There have been many examples of companies that run a marketing campaign that is too successful in getting new users and thus overloads their systems. To add this effect into the future growth plan, we developed a spreadsheet-based model that parameterizes the expected increase in load. The parameters should be expressed in a form similar to the justification for the campaign generated by the marketing people. These parameters include the duration of the campaign (L); a scale factor related to the impact or reach (S); a residual level which is the long-term increase in use load resulting from this campaign (r); and a delay that sets the starting point for the campaign in the model (d).

The spreadsheet available at http://www.sun.com/blueprints/tools uses a formula that estimates the marketing reach of a campaign. This formula is appropriate in some circumstances; however, other formulas may better represent a marketing impact depending on your environment. Most formulas can be easily implemented in a spreadsheet to work with the rest of this procedure. The following example provides a brief description of the formula the spreadsheet uses for a marketing campaign.

Because it may be difficult to understand the mathematics implemented by the spreadsheet, the following formula may be helpful in understanding how the spreadsheet was derived. However, it is not necessary to understand this formula to use the spreadsheet model.

The load change (L_t) caused by the marketing effects at time t is:

$$L_t = L_0 S\left(\frac{e^{-L}L^{t-d}}{(t-d)!}\right) + r$$

TABLE 4-4 shows an example of the results of the spreadsheet implementation using the following values:

- Duration (L) = 3.4 months
- Scale (S) = 3.0 times
- Residual level (r) = 1.2 times
- Delay (d) = 4.0 months

TABLE 4-4 shows an example of marketing campaign load boost factors.

TABLE 4-4   Marketing Campaign Load Boost Factors

Month	Growth Factor
1	1.00
2	1.00
3	1.00
4	1.30
5	1.54
6	1.78
7	1.86
8	1.76
9	1.58
10	1.41
11	1.30
12	1.24
13	1.22
14	1.21
15	1.20

FIGURE 4-9 graphically represents the marketing campaign load boost.

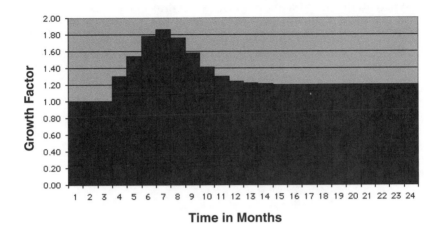

FIGURE 4-9   Graph of Marketing Campaign Boost

In FIGURE 4-9, a marketing campaign starts in the fourth month to counteract the expected seasonal drop in load level. It continues for four months, then the memories fade away and a residual increased level of activity is seen. The short-term and residual gain should be something that the marketing department uses to justify the campaign in the first place, so its impact can be modelled in the same way as its impact on the business. The campaign is not repeated in the second year; the chart in FIGURE 4-9 shows why it was not needed. In practice, many smaller marketing boosts may be modelled rather than one large boost.

Combined Load Estimate

When all the load increasing factors are multiplied together (i.e., the seasonal effect, geometric exponential workload growth, and marketing boost), a combined growth factor will result. In this case (see TABLE 4-5), you can see that the final end point is about 30 times the start point after two years, and that this boost mostly occurs at the end, where seasonal and geometric exponential growth combine.

TABLE 4-5 Combined Load Calculation

Month	Workload	Marketing	Seasonal	Total Load
1	1.14	1.00	0.89	1.02
2	1.31	1.00	1.00	1.31
3	1.50	1.00	0.61	0.92
4	1.72	1.30	0.56	1.24
5	1.97	1.54	0.44	1.35
6	2.25	1.78	0.39	1.56
7	2.58	1.86	0.33	1.59
8	2.95	1.76	0.33	1.73
9	3.38	1.58	0.78	4.15
10	3.86	1.41	0.89	4.86
11	4.42	1.30	1.00	5.77
12	5.06	1.24	1.00	6.30
13	5.80	1.22	0.89	6.27
14	6.63	1.21	0.72	5.78
15	7.59	1.20	0.61	5.58
16	8.69	1.20	0.56	5.80
17	9.95	1.20	0.44	5.31
18	11.39	1.20	0.39	5.32
19	13.04	1.20	0.33	5.22
20	14.93	1.20	0.33	5.97
21	17.09	1.20	0.78	15.95
22	19.56	1.20	0.89	20.86
23	22.39	1.20	1.00	26.87
24	25.63	1.20	1.00	30.75

FIGURE 4-10 graphically shows the combined load.

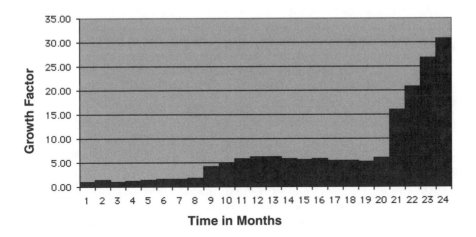

FIGURE 4-10 Chart of Combined Load

Modelling Capacity

As with load, the factors that affect capacity can be separately computed in a spreadsheet and then combined to get a combined capacity estimation. Many capacity measurements can be modelled. The two influences on capacity shown below are efficiency variations and capacity increases.

- Efficiency variations cover all other factors that increase effective capacity. This includes application and system tuning, as well as the removal of load from the bottleneck by parallelizing or offloading functionality. Keep in mind that any load-reducing effects reflected in the load total should not be reflected by the efficiency variations.

- Capacity increases include anything that allows increased capacity because of upgrades to the bottleneck. Since the bottleneck in this example is the CPU, anything that affects the total CPU power of the machine is considered a capacity increase. These include processor upgrades, as well as OS upgrades and database upgrades (which may use the existing processor power more or less effectively).

Efficiency Variations

The model for load is based on a relatively constant resource usage per transaction of the resource causing the bottleneck. In the example above, CPU usage is the bottleneck, and the load model is based on constant average CPU usage per transaction. Large changes in the application or transaction mix need to be accounted for in the scenario plan. Ideally, performance tuning the application or offloading some functionality to other systems will reduce the amount of bottle-necked resource used per transaction every few months, so that a schedule for expected (or desired) changes in the application efficiency can be laid out as part of the model and recorded in the spreadsheet.

TABLE 4-6 shows the effects of heavy application tuning on the CPU usage per transaction in the above example. Although these results may be unrepresentative of what can be achieved in many situations, it is sometimes possible to achieve a four- or five-fold performance improvement (like the one shown here) by tuning customer applications or databases. When planning for future capacity, it is important to talk to the programmers, consultants, or DBAs tuning the system in question to get an accurate expectation of the amount of tuning that can be achieved.

The second column of TABLE 4-6 shows the amount of relative CPU usage per transaction (baselining the initial value at 1). The third column shows the inverse of this, which represents the application's efficiency in terms of how much more efficient the tuned application is compared to the untuned one.

TABLE 4-6 Application CPU Usage per Transaction

Month	Application CPU Usage per Transaction	Application Efficiency Factor (Transactions per CPU)
1	1.00	1
2	1.00	1
3	0.80	1.25
4	0.80	1.25
5	0.90	1.11
6	0.90	1.11
7	0.90	1.11
8	0.70	1.43
9	0.70	1.43
10	0.55	1.82
11	0.55	1.82
12	0.55	1.82

TABLE 4-6   Application CPU Usage per Transaction *(Continued)*

Month	Application CPU Usage per Transaction	Application Efficiency Factor (Transactions per CPU)
13	0.55	1.82
14	0.50	2
15	0.50	2
16	0.50	2
17	0.30	3.33
18	0.30	3.33
19	0.30	3.33
20	0.20	5
21	0.20	5
22	0.20	5
23	0.15	6.67
24	0.15	6.67

The factors in TABLE 4-6 are plotted in FIGURE 4-11.

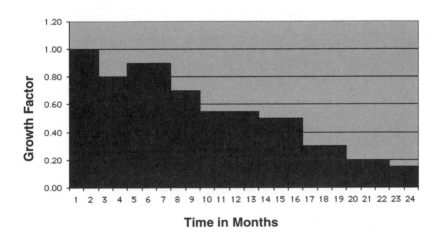

FIGURE 4-11 Chart of Application CPU Usage per Transaction

To counteract the increased load levels, the application is tuned and the hardware is upgraded. If your initial application is untuned, it may be possible to incrementally achieve a four- or five-fold improvement by tuning and reimplementing custom applications and databases over several years. In the chart shown in FIGURE 4-11, database tuning or application software upgrades give the first two gains; then there is a reversal as a new, more complex user interface is introduced. This makes the users happier but adds to the load. After a while, several more tuning improvements are made, until after two years, the computer resources used per transaction is reduced to 15% of that at the start.

Capacity Increases

Hardware vendors can supply capacity increases in the form of more efficient operating systems, more CPUs, faster CPUs, or new generations of systems. Systems that depend on a database can include the database version here as part of the platform efficiency. This causes a series of steps (see TABLE 4-7) that are captured in the spreadsheet and shown graphically in FIGURE 4-12. The performance factors must be estimated from experience with the application in use and standard industry benchmarks; the factors shown here were made up for illustrative purposes. Appendix A, "Sun Constant Performance Metrics," shows some performance numbers for various machines that may be appropriate for projecting the capacity of new hardware.

TABLE 4-7   Hardware Upgrade Capacity Increase Factors

Month	Comment	Performance Assuming 70% Utilization	Factor Assuming 70% Utilization	Factor Assuming 100% Utilization
1	CPU E6K 12 x 333 MHz + 4 MB	1000	1.0	1.43
2		1000	1.0	1.43
3		1000	1.0	1.43
4		1000	1.0	1.43
5	CPU E6K 16 x 333 MHz + 4 MB	1200	1.2	1.71
6		1200	1.2	1.71
7		1200	1.2	1.71
8	Oracle 8 Upgrade	1400	1.4	2.00
9		1400	1.4	2.00
10	CPU E6K 20 x 333 MHz + 4MB	1600	1.6	2.29
11		1600	1.6	2.29
12	CPU E6K 24 x 333 MHz + 4MB	1800	1.8	2.57
13		1800	1.8	2.57

TABLE 4-7   Hardware Upgrade Capacity Increase Factors *(Continued)*

Month	Comment	Performance Assuming 70% Utilization	Factor Assuming 70% Utilization	Factor Assuming 100% Utilization
14	Solaris 7 OE upgrade	2000	2.0	2.86
15		2000	2.0	2.86
16		2000	2.0	2.86
17		2000	2.0	2.86
18		2000	2.0	2.86
19		2000	2.0	2.86
20	CPU E10K 40 x 400 MHz + 8 MB	3000	3.0	4.29
21		3000	3.0	4.29
22	Solaris OE/Oracle 64-bit upgrade	3500	3.5	5.00
23		3500	3.5	5.00
24		3500	3.5	5.00

A notional level of 70% capacity utilization was also factored in, assuming that the system was 70% busy before the start.

For the graph in FIGURE 4-12, some system configurations and performance factors were invented.

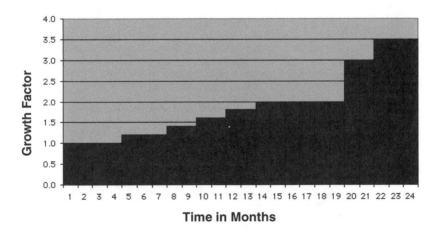

FIGURE 4-12 Chart of Hardware Upgrade Capacity Increase Factors

In TABLE 4-7, the third column shows the CPU utilization in each month. This assumes a start point, which for this case is entered into the spreadsheet as 70% busy at month zero. The utilization is calculated by taking into account all the different growth factors explained in the next section.

Combined Capacity Estimate

The combined effects of the capacity increases can be computed in a manner similar to combining the load increases as shown in TABLE 4-8. This computation can easily be done with the spreadsheet. The final column shows the utilization each month, which consists of the total load (from TABLE 4-5), divided by the capability computed below.

TABLE 4-8   Combined Capability Calculation

Month	Hardware Capacity Factor Assuming 100% Utilization	Application Efficiency	Capability (Hardware Capacity Times Application Efficiency	Utilization (Load/ Capability)
1	1.43	1	1.43	71%
2	1.43	1	1.43	92%
3	1.43	1.25	1.79	51%
4	1.43	1.25	1.79	69%
5	1.71	1.11	1.90	71%
6	1.71	1.11	1.90	82%
7	1.71	1.11	1.90	84%
8	2.00	1.43	2.86	60%
9	2.00	1.43	2.86	145%
10	2.29	1.82	4.16	117%
11	2.29	1.82	4.16	139%
12	2.57	1.82	4.68	135%
13	2.57	1.82	4.68	134%
14	2.86	2	5.71	101%
15	2.86	2	5.71	98%
16	2.86	2	5.71	101%
17	2.86	3.33	9.52	56%
18	2.86	3.33	9.52	56%
19	2.86	3.33	9.52	55%

TABLE 4-8   Combined Capability Calculation *(Continued)*

Month	Hardware Capacity Factor Assuming 100% Utilization	Application Efficiency	Capability (Hardware Capacity Times Application Efficiency	Utilization (Load/ Capability)
20	4.29	5	21.43	28%
21	4.29	5	21.43	74%
22	5.00	5	25.00	83%
23	5.00	6.67	33.33	81%
24	5.00	6.67	33.33	92%

The combination of efficiency and hardware capacity upgrades can be plotted on the same axis (FIGURE 4-13) to see if the system is capable of sustaining the load.

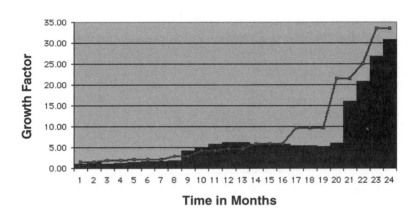

FIGURE 4-13 Chart of Combined Load vs. Capability

The plot in FIGURE 4-13 shows that the combination of a marketing campaign and the seasonal boost overloads the server at peak times through the first Christmas period. If this model is correct, something else needs to be done to sustain this future business scenario. Either a faster system could be installed earlier, or more efficiency could be squeezed out of the system. However, another option is that the work itself could be split in some way, possibly by functional or geographical aspects. If you were modelling the front-end http servers, search engines, or application servers, you could increase the number of servers. It is much harder to split up a back-end database.

Tweaking the Model

The example spreadsheet used previously has been carefully tweaked to give a capability that tracks the load level reasonably well. When you first enter your own data and estimates into the spreadsheet, you will probably find that you have a very poor fit after the first few months. You will need to spend some time tweaking the parameters in the model, trying out alternative *what-if* scenarios until you are happy that your assumptions make sense. When manipulating the data, bear in mind that the analysis is based on peak loads, not average loads. If you take measurements at intervals of a few minutes, they can be averaged; but as soon as you zoom out to considering intervals of an hour or more, you want to know the peak level during that hour and the peak hour during the day.

Predicting Tomorrow

With all this data and some idea of the typical daily profile, you can predict the next few days in detail, then monitor the real load level to see how close you get. You can simply combine the weekly and monthly predictions to get an estimate of the load level over the next week. The monthly data is based on the peak for the whole month, and it could occur at any time during the month; so, you could simply assume that the monthly peak could occur on any of the days that coincide with the weekly peak. For example, if the weekly peak is a Monday, then the monthly peak could occur on any Monday in the month. This gives you a slightly conservative estimate.

Fitting the Model to the Data by Tweaking

For a large Internet site, the daily Web traffic was analyzed to pick out the cgi-bin transactions that caused the back-end database to be invoked. These counts were further reduced to obtain the busiest day in each month for an 18-month period. This set of numbers was then fitted into the spreadsheet-based model, taking into account geometric exponential growth, seasonality, and marketing-related variations.

1. **Add the measured data to the planning spreadsheet.**

   The first step is to make a new graph that shows the measured data and the predicted data, including a table showing the proportional difference (the error in the fit) between the two.

2. **Tweak the geometric exponential growth.**

   Set the workload growth parameters shown in TABLE 4-3 to get a first approximation of the overall long-term growth rate.

3. **Tweak the seasonality.**

   Look at the difference factors calculated in the first step. Where two months a year apart are out by a similar factor, add that factor to the seasonal load variation estimates in TABLE 4-2.

4. **Carry on tweaking.**

   Go back and vary the exponential growth factor to try and get the difference to match better year after year, and tweak the seasonality factors until as many months as possible have a good match. Go around this loop several times.

5. **Set up marketing factors.**

   Anything that is not explained by growth and does not repeat from year to year is taken care of as if it is due to marketing awareness bias. The marketing factors can be set up to zero out the difference factors.

6. **Keep tinkering.**

   Make sure that you don't have marketing factors that repeat year after year; these values should be moved to be seasonal.

7. **Predict the next few months.**

   Come up with estimates for the next few months, compare the estimates with reality as they occur, and refine the model to take new data into account.

Summary

Spreadsheet-based models are a good starting point, but are extremely limited and can be clumsy to use and extend. As soon as you want to model more than one system or a mixture of several kinds of workloads, the mathematics become too complex for a spreadsheet. There are several tools that can handle multiclass and multisystem models.

It is easier to model CPU utilization than disk capacity and performance, but large disk subsystems are expensive and may be the primary bottleneck of your application. In the next chapter, we introduce a simplified model of disk performance that can cope with complex disk subsystems.

Capacity Estimation

The four key components of any system can be grouped into CPU, memory, disks, and networks. Each of these need to be examined to determine the capacity available and the utilization of that capacity. By identifying the primary bottleneck, the examination shows where the system can be expected to run out of headroom first.

Earlier in this book, we assumed that capacity and utilization were easy to obtain for bottleneck estimation. In practice, getting those values may actually be more complex, so this chapter examines the problems in more detail.

Overview

CPU capacity is quite easy to estimate from numbers obtained with vmstat and sar. Sum the user and system time to calculate CPU utilization, leaving the idle and wait for I/O time as the remaining headroom. The underlying data is inaccurate at low utilization levels. As long as the utilization is above 10% busy, the reported utilization is good enough for the purposes of capacity estimation. The Sun BluePrints book *Resource Management* discusses the sources of error in more detail in the Measurements and Workload Analysis chapters.

You measure network capacity by using the byte level throughput counters and applying some configuration knowledge of what bit rate the interface is running at. These counters are not printed by standard system utilities because they are device-dependent. The SE toolkit[1] nx.se script formats them nicely, or the command netstat -k displays the raw data for the hme, qfe, and ge interfaces. The Solaris 8 OE adds the kstat command, which obtains and processes these counters more conveniently.

Memory capacity is difficult to estimate in older Solaris OE releases. The priority_paging option improves memory usage characteristics and has been backported to the Solaris 2.5.1 and 2.6 OEs. The priority_paging option is available in the appropriate kernel update patch. Solaris 7 OE includes this code as

---

1. The latest SE toolkit is available at http://www.setoolkit.com.

standard, but it must be enabled explicitly in /etc/system. Solaris 7 OE also add
a new option to vmstat to break down the reasons for paging. If executable code i
being paged out, you definitely need more memory; however, if just file cache is
being paged out and freed, you have no problem. Solaris 8 OE changes the memor
management subsystem in several ways to make paging much simpler to
understand. There is no need for priority paging in Solaris 8 OE because a more
sophisticated scheme is used by default. You should see no scanning, a lot more
page reclaims, and a much higher free memory value reported by vmstat. With
Solaris 8 OE, the free value in vmstat can be used reliably as a measure of how
much memory is free for new applications to use on a system, so it solves the
capacity estimation problem.

Disk capacity estimation has become very complex because of too many different
types of CPUs with varying scalability characteristics. Consequently, these varying
characteristics create complicated disk subsystems. The following sections give
examples of system resource modelling and look at the problem of capacity plannin
for CPU and disk subsystems in detail.

System Measurement Frames

The time period measured for the utilization of system resources is key to accurate
system resource modelling. By choosing a representative period that accurately
reflects system usage, you can use the model to project system utilization and load
planning impacts through to the applied system changes.

A system can be modelled as a whole or broken down into individual services to
build separate models for different functions. One primary example of this is an
online transaction processing (OLTP) order processing system that runs backups
nightly and has an integrated database report generation system. Separate SLAs
might exist for system performance during system maintenance tasks, system
performance during business hours, and the length of time allowed for system
maintenance tasks and database batch report runs. In this scenario, models should
be created showing interactive performance inside and outside the allowed
maintenance window, as well as the "batch load" performance of the backup system
and reporting system.

Resource management schemes, such as processor sets and SRM software, can be
used to control the backup and reporting systems to reduce impact on OLTP. In
addition, these schemes can be used to reduce the impact of transaction processing
to assure that backups and reports can be completed in the assigned processing
windows. At this point in the capacity and performance management cycle, intimate
knowledge of the business system being modelled is required to prioritize the
workload that might be competing for system resources. In this simplified example

of system utilization (FIGURE 5-1), a basic "consumer shift" of customer interaction between 8:00 a.m. and 6:00 p.m. and a maintenance task shift between 1:00 a.m. and 4:00 a.m. are easily recognized.

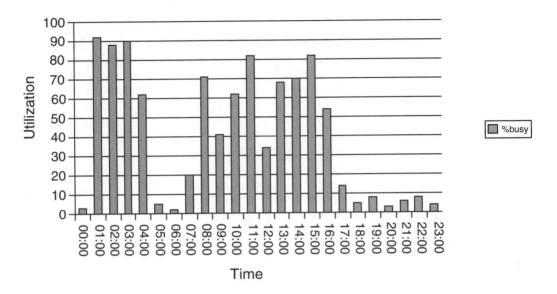

FIGURE 5-1   Graph of CPU Utilization Over a 24-Hour Sample

The first step in building a model is to choose an appropriate sample period. For consumer shift processing, SLAs are most likely defined for transactional volumes and system response time. The sample period should reflect the maximum period of time for which degraded system performance is to be tolerated, with a critical threshold of maximum degradation to be allowed. In an online processing system that has direct interaction with the paying customer of the business, the sample period could be as low as one minute. These samples are used for analysis and tracking and are averaged into longer time frames for summarized reporting.

In a batch processing environment such as scheduled report generation and system backups, the high system utilization and resulting system OLTP performance degradation are not exposed to the end-user and they are actually expected and planned for. System batch processing that occurs outside the consumer-exposed processing window should fully utilize system resources to shorten the runtime of the batch processes. For this reason, SLA-defined thresholds for system utilization and transactional performance are not in effect for batch processing windows.

Overlapping batch processing windows and transactional processing should be avoided where possible. Batch reports, database record purging, system backups, and other batch system maintenance should be scheduled into time windows isolated from periods of customer interaction. In systems where customer interaction is necessary 24 hours a day, 7 days a week, strict and balanced system resource management is required.

For systems where transaction processing overlaps the maintenance window, more complex modelling is required. Capacity management suites such as TeamQuest and BMC's Best/1 are capable of accurately separating the workload processing and modelling the resource conflicts of multiple workloads competing for system resources. With basic scripting, simple models using system utilities such as mpstat can be used in conjunction with processor sets to monitor shared workload environments to collect and present the system resource data. In this example (FIGURE 5-2), the batch report generation system is operating around the clock, the OLTP system is operating on a peak shift of 8:00 a.m. to 6:00 p.m., and system maintenance tasks are competing for system resources during the system maintenance window of 1:00 a.m. to 4:00 a.m.

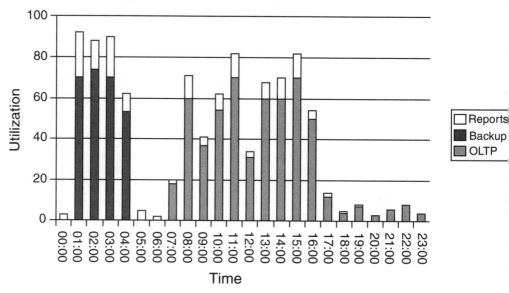

FIGURE 5-2   Graph of CPU Utilization by Workload

One immediate change to workload scheduling can be derived from this graph. There appear to be batch reports running during the system maintenance window. By moving these batch reports outside the defined maintenance window and creating a defined shift for reporting tasks (see FIGURE 5-3), we can enforce resource management through a published scheduling policy. System utilization is then controlled through policy, rather than system enforcement. This simple approach is often the most cost-effective (free) at the onset, but can result in underutilized system resources when workloads could otherwise coexist without contention or with contention minimized through the proper use of resource management tools.

To illustrate this case, midday reports are allowed between 12:00 p.m. and 1:00 p.m. for hourly summary tracking of morning transactions; all other report generation is assigned to the 6:00 p.m. to 0:00 a.m. window.

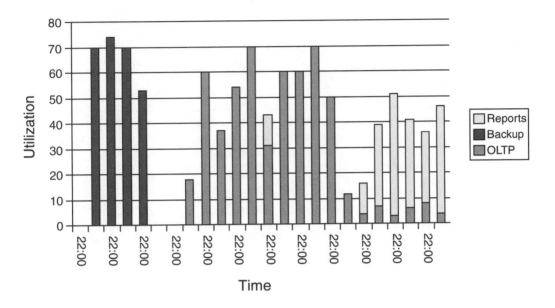

FIGURE 5-3   Graph of CPU Utilization After Load Balancing

Isolating the different system processing tasks greatly simplifies the implementation of monitoring tools and system resource data collection.

Sun Constant Performance Metric (SCPM) Value Capacity Planning

At Sun, we have been using our own capacity estimation method (developed by Brian Wong), which is based on historical mainframe capacity planning methods and has been refined through many years of internal and customer engagements. Brian's method is commonly referred to as the "M-value process," after the traditional mainframe performance metric. By creating a series of generic terms to define *work* on a computer and creating metrics for a volume of work, it is possible to quantify several statistics. These statistics describe the capacity of the machine platform, as well as the performance characteristics of a given workload on a machine.

The basis of this method is a performance metric describing the quantity of work that a particular system configuration is capable of processing. This number, called the Sun constant performance metric (SCPM), represents the relative performance of a given server. The metric by which an SCPM is scaled is called the quanta (Q). SCPMs are adjusted based on measured performance values using predictable benchmarks. In addition, SCPMs are a real-world estimation of Amdahl's Law applied to system architectures and operating system versions for cases of regular, predictable, and *normal* workloads. Occasionally, significant patches may influence the scalability of an operating system; in that case, SCPM values must be adjusted for the relevant platforms. The trends in SCPM values across the operating system and patch versions can be examined and used when upgrading. Examining these trends can provide guidance for predicting the impact that upgrade modifications might have on system performance. See Appendix A, "Sun Constant Performance Metrics," for a complete list of comparative system capacity estimations for Solaris OE versions 2.5, 2.5.1, 2.6, 7, and 8.

Any metric that relates to your particular application's performance characteristics on a given hardware platform can be used. Examples of possible alternatives include SPECrate, SPECint, TPC benchmark numbers, and benchmarks from software vendors such as SAP, Baan, and Peoplesoft. This method has proven valid, with accuracy dependent on the applicability of the chosen comparative performance metric to your particular workload.

Rather than using the supplied, somewhat conservative estimations of multiprocessor scalability, you can measure the workload being projected for parallelization with the SCPM values, providing relative CPU performance metrics for CPU and architecture changes. Measuring the potential parallelization of your particular workload provides a more accurate model of the performance characteristics of your workload, which results in more accurate projections of system resource utilization.

Amdahl's Law

Amdahl's Law provides the calculations for predicting the benefit of running a workload on a scalable multiprocessor environment. We can apply a simplified set of calculations based on Amdahl's Law to project the scalability of our workload.

The first result of interest is the speed-up factor of your measured workload. The speed-up factor is a calculated variable for your workload; it describes the capability of your application to do work in parallel while taking advantage of additional processors. The parallelization is limited by finite resource contention and "serial operations" that cannot take advantage of additional processors and could actually degrade workload throughput. Application of Amdahl's Law measures CPU architectures and presumes that there are no bottlenecks in the disk or network subsystems and that memory is adequate to process the workload without starvation.

The speed-up of a workload is calculated from measurements taken with a chosen workload running on one CPU and that same workload running on several CPUs. It is best to use a series of measurements of speed-up, using a logical progression of CPU counts reflecting the likely upgrade path to your system architecture (1, 2, 4, 8, 12, 16, °…). Speed-up is calculated using the time taken to accomplish a defined set of representative transactions. The following formula is used for a measured time (T) to do the same transactions with one CPU and n CPUs:

$$Speed-up_{(n)} = \frac{T_{(1)}}{T_{(n)}}$$

By applying some simple algebra to this formula and using a fixed time frame for measurement, we can calculate speed-up from the throughput of transactions with varying quantities of CPUs. The following formula is used for throughput in number of transactions (N) of a given workload run over a fixed period of time on one CPU and n CPUs:

$$Speed-up_{(n)} = \frac{N_{(n)}}{N_{(1)}}$$

Geometric Scalability

The speed-up factor that is calculated with a single CPU and two CPUs can be used to calculate the scalability factor (S) of a given workload. The scalability factor is a constant (associated with the measured workload), describing how well the workload will operate on a machine containing more of the same type of CPU. The following formula demonstrates that the scalability factor represents the percentage of the workload that is parallelized, and not the finite resource constrained:

$$S = Speed-up_{(2)} - 1$$

The scalability of a given machine for a given workload can be predicted with the scalability factor, and by compounding the scalability for a given number of CPUs. The scalability factor may be reduced if there is resource contention. Adding CPUs will increase the contention, thereby reducing the percentage gains. The following formula is used for a machine with n CPUs, a scalability factor of S, and a measured throughput of $T_{(1)}$ with a single CPU:

$$T(n) = T(1) + (S \times T(1)) + (S^2 \times T(1)) + \dots + (S^{n-1} \times T(1))$$

The graph in FIGURE 5-4 shows scalability factors of 100% (linear scalability), 99.5%, 98%, and 70% for an eight-CPU architecture; in addition, the graph shows the relative performance increase of adding CPUs. Lower scalability factors can influence system architecture decisions toward *wider* server architectures, with more smaller servers combined to provide the end-user service. Higher scalability factors can help influence architecture decisions to *deeper* server architectures, with fewer larger machines providing the service.

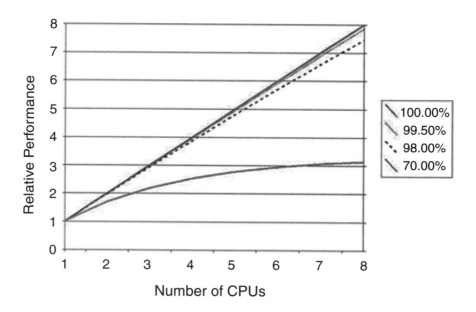

FIGURE 5-4 Eight-CPU Geometric Scalability

Deeper architectures are generally easier to manage and can lower infrastructure and support costs. With deeper architectures, a direct relationship is established between the scalability of an application architecture and the potential total cost of ownership (TCO). With lower scalability factors, the progressively lower increase in performance benefit of adding additional CPUs (see FIGURE 5-5) can outweigh the potential savings in TCO of managing fewer systems. Larger system architectures generally provide more reliability and serviceability features. For example, the "N+1" power and cooling subsystems supply enough power and cooling capabilities to survive a single component failure, as well as other redundant components, redundant data paths, and redundant peripheral adapters. Consequently, the N+1 power and cooling subsystems increase the potential system availability.

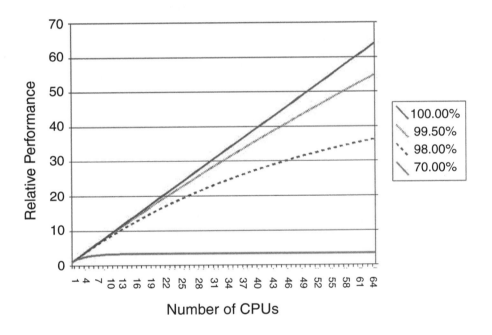

FIGURE 5-5 64-CPU Geometric Scalability

The scalability of any particular software on a particular server might display nongeometric scalability characteristics. For most *normal* workloads that we have measured, the variances from the geometric scalability curves are minimal. Factors that might cause a significant variance include:

- *CPU cache/code efficiency* – If the whole of, or a significant portion of, the server application's execution can occur from within the CPU cache without preemption or flushing of the CPU cache, the scalability of that application will "bump up" when the most frequently accessed pieces of an application can fit within the combined CPU caches and across a number of CPUs.

- *Limits to application software threading* – If the application software is incapable of threading, or running as multiple instances, or has some static limit to the number of server threads utilized to provide the service, additional CPUs will not generally add significant increases in throughput or improved response times.

- *Finite resource consumption* – If the software consumes a finite set of one or more resources, at some point, the contention for resources could actually degrade the overall throughput and increase application response times. The reason is that too many threads or instances of a server application could be competing with each other. Examples of resource contention areas include locking mechanisms for exclusive access to resources, single pipelines for data I/O, and even hardware device and device driver limitations.

Measuring Utilization

The SCPM capacity planning process applies the basis of the Utilization Law to measure how much of a server's resources are being consumed during a sample measured period. The Utilization Law[1] is defined as:

During a period of time (T), tasks are submitted to the server. The server processes the tasks, and the tasks have a finite conclusion. Component resources (CPU time, disk I/Os per second) within the server have a finite capacity. Processing consumes measurable resources in the server platform. An observer of the server during the observed time frame can identify the:

- Amount of time during the observed time frame that the server resource component is busy processing tasks (B)
- Number of tasks completed during the time frame (C)

These measurements result in the following calculations:

- Output rate or throughput of the server measured in tasks per unit of time.

    Throughput = $C \div T$

- Average service time to complete a computing task:

    Service Time = $B \div C$

- Percentage of the observation period that the server resource component is processing tasks, called the utilization of the server:

    Percent Utilization = $B \div T$

From this application of the Utilization Law, we can state empirical measured metrics to characterize the measured workload such as:

1. "Queueing in Networks of Computers," <u>American Scientist</u> 79, 3 (May-June 1991).

For a sustained level of 12,000 catalog lookup queries per hour, CPU utilization was measured as 62% busy and disk utilization was measured as 22% busy.

Fortunately, common system reporting utilities report percent utilization, but it is still useful to understand the underlying computations.

SCPM Measurement

In the SCPM process, a unit of work is called a quanta (Q). Systems that contain potential for doing work are represented by (M), which is a multiple of a quanta. The amount of work being done on a machine is the quanta consumed (QC), or measured system utilization multiplied by (M). FIGURE 5-6 is an example of the SCPM process.

```
heisenberg% sar -s 08:00 -e 16:00 -i 3600 -f /var/adm/sa/sa27

SunOS heisenberg 5.8 sun4u     03/27/00

08:00:00    %usr    %sys    %wio    %idle
09:00:00     24       9       0      66
10:00:00     34      13       0      53
11:00:00     34      12       0      54
12:00:00     21       9       0      70
13:00:00     52      21       0      27
14:00:00     61      27       0      12
15:00:00     58      24       0      18
16:00:00     54      23       0      23

Average      42      17       0      41
```

FIGURE 5-6   Sample SCPM Process

This description of the SCPM process has been simplified for this exercise. There are many other considerations in performance baselining with the SCPM process, but the basic concept behind the process is fairly easy to understand. By measuring real workloads and their relative disk I/O, CPU, memory, and network consumption, you can predict the effective resource consumption of that workload. You can also project resource consumption into other SCPM-rated platforms or modify the volumes of work being performed within the model.

In this example, hourly samples of CPU utilization were extracted from the system sar data to represent a given shift. The start time is 8:00 a.m., and the end time is 5:00 p.m., or 16:00 plus the hour of the sample. The sample interval is 3600 seconds or one hour. The output of sar can easily be imported into a spreadsheet for further calculations (see FIGURE 5-7).

	A	B	C	D	E	F	G
1							
2	08:00:00	%usr	%sys	%busy	QC		
3	09:00:00	24	9	33	9793.41		
4	10:00:00	34	13	47	13948.19		
5	11:00:00	34	12	46	13651.42		
6	12:00:00	21	9	30	8903.1		
7	13:00:00	52	21	73	21664.21		
8	14:00:00	61	27	88	26115.76		
9	15:00:00	58	24	82	24335.14		
10	16:00:00	54	23	77	22851.29		
11							
12	Average	42	17	59	17509.43		
13							
14	Server Description	E4500 – 12x 250Mhz / 4M Processors					
15	SCPM	29677					
16	Shift QC	17509.43					
17	Peak Hour QC	26115.76					
18							
19							

FIGURE 5-7   Sample Spreadsheet of SCPM Process

By adding the %usr and %sys columns from the sar-generated data, we now have the %busy for each sample period and a shift average. The %wio column is not considered for this exercise, because %wio indicates the time that the CPUs were waiting, and not processing. This process measures workload processing or "think time"; thus, waiting on disk activity would be considered "idle." The %wio is always a function of the disk subsystem and will be minimized elsewhere in the capacity planning process.

If our target peak hour utilization has been defined in the KPI document to be 70%, we are showing four hours of utilization over the target. This can be presented graphically (FIGURE 5-8) for the executive summary of the SLA and KPI reports.

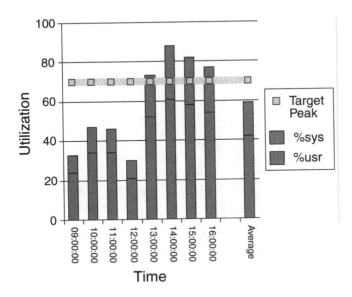

FIGURE 5-8   CPU Utilization Graph

We can also project the measured system utilization into the system SCPM value to produce the quanta consumed (QC) over time (see FIGURE 5-9). This representation can sometimes be easier to understand than percentage utilization graphs because it focuses more on the goal of system resource consumption rather than on the used/ unused resources of a system. The utilization-based graph can sometimes be interpreted as showing that there is plenty of system capacity, despite the presentation of utilization exceeding the stated goals of the KPI. These graphic representations can be included in an executive overview document for SLA and KPI review.

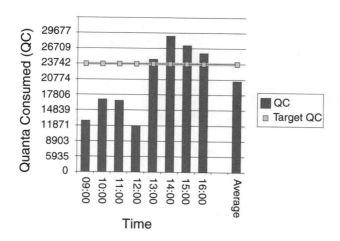

FIGURE 5-9 System Quanta Consumed Graph

We can now project the measured workload into a different platform, projecting the system utilization of that system. In this example (FIGURE 5-10), we upgrade from our measured platform (an E4500 with 12 × 250 MHz, 4MB cache CPUs) to a Sun Enterprise 4500 server with 12 × 400 MHz, 8 MB cache CPUs. The upgraded system will have a predicted utilization of (QC ÷ M).

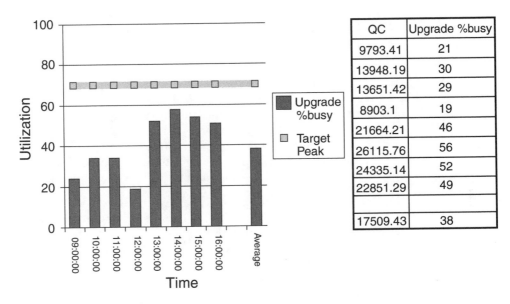

QC	Upgrade %busy
9793.41	21
13948.19	30
13651.42	29
8903.1	19
21664.21	46
26115.76	56
24335.14	52
22851.29	49
17509.43	38

FIGURE 5-10 Upgraded CPU Utilization Graph

If we divide the QC on a given platform by the number of users accomplishing that work, we now have the quanta consumed per user (QC ÷ User). You can then compute the number of users that a given machine will support:

Total Users Supported = (SCPM × Target Utilization) ÷ (QC ÷ User)

As part of load planning or server consolidation exercises, the (QC ÷ User) can help us plan for future growth and load changes within our model and will project system utilization for a variety of possible scenarios.

Measuring Disk Storage Capacity

Capacity planning with SCPM values provides a simple method for measuring, reporting, and predicting consumption of CPU resources. This same method can be modified slightly and applied to disk subsystems. By measuring the transactions and utilization of the disk subsystems and projecting against the capabilities of the subsystem being consumed, we can create a model for storage capacity planning.

The first measurable metric used in this method is the total number of disk I/O activities per unit of time (generally averaged out to one second and referred to as I/Os per second, or IOPS) generated by the measured workload. This metric can be measured and reported with `iostat`, `sar`, SunMC, or other system monitoring tools. It is critical to the validity and accuracy of these metrics that the measurements be taken during a steady state, or a time frame when the flow of transactions is relatively constant and indicative of a period of normal user activity.

The activity being measured is only related to disk activity, so data generated by tools that report tape drive, Network File System (NFS), or CD-ROM activity must be "cleaned" before being used for capacity planning. The number of disk activities is measured and reported for total disk activity, including reads and writes (S), as well as individual measurements for disk read activities (S_R) and disk write activities (S_W).

For the measured period shown in TABLE 5-1, the total number of disk activities (S) was 182, which is the sum of the r+w/s column, excluding the `nfs1` and `st11` devices (NFS and tape drive utilization).

TABLE 5-1   `sar` Disk Output

00:00:01	device	%busy	avque	r+w/s	blks/s	avwait	avserv
Avg	nfs1	0	0.0	0	0	0.0	0.0
	sd0	1	0.0	12	19	0.3	79.9
	sd1	0	0.0	14	22	0.0	30.6
	sd2	1	0.0	8	13	0.3	79.9
	sd3	0	0.0	9	15	0.0	30.6
	sd4	1	0.0	11	18	0.3	79.9
	sd5	0	0.0	6	8	0.0	30.6
	sd41	31	0.4	34	41	0.5	22.2
	sd42	14	0.2	16	19	0.2	24.1
	sd68	19	0.2	21	25	0.2	23.8

TABLE 5-1   sar Disk Output *(Continued)*

00:00:01 device	%busy	avque	r+w/s	blks/s	avwait	avserv
sd69	19	0.2	21	26	0.2	22.9
sd70	6	0.1	14	17	0.2	18.1
sd71	13	4.3	16	19	0.2	24.1
st11	2	4.3	122	484	2.3	332.2

The number of disk activities during the measured period can be referenced in relation to the service levels provided in that sample time. By dividing the disk activities per second by the transactional rate in transactions per second (TPS), we can compute a metric indicating the disk activity per transaction, which is a vital indication of the relative disk resource consumption of the application:

Reads per Transaction = S_R / TPS

Writes per Transaction = S_W / TPS

Disk Activities per Transaction = S / TPS

The disk activity can also be computed in relation to the SCPM QC to acquire the relative disk I/O content (*R*) value of the measured workload. This metric describes the relationship of disk activity to CPU resources consumed, independent of the server platform on which the workload was measured. For a given amount of work done by the CPUs, the following formula shows that we can now associate a relative quantity of work done by the disk subsystem to support that processing:

R = S ÷ QC

The relative disk I/O content for a given workload should remain almost constant. Changes to a workload (new features, new data structures) can change the R value for a workload, and should trigger a new measurement cycle to establish a new baseline. The historic measurements should be maintained relative to the established software change management process to document the performance characteristic changes induced by changes in the service application and server architecture.

Total disk throughput (T_{Disk}) can be computed by multiplying the disk I/O size of the given storage subsystem (raw disk access size, or file system block size) times the number of disk activities (*S*) for the system. This number does not take into account the metadata activity (ACL, inode, directory lookup) and will be slightly higher than the measured activity. The size of the datasets generally increases faster than the volume of metadata activity (files grow faster than the number of individual files grows), so in this case, we choose to err on the side of safety and overestimate the maximum required disk throughput. As the system grows, this value should approach reality and become more accurate as we calibrate the measured average I/O sizes against the data access I/O size.

Increased cache efficiencies provided by volume management, file systems, applications, database software improvements, and database query optimizations can significantly reduce the disk I/O required to complete a transaction. New features and functionality in the software architecture can increase the processing power necessary to complete a transaction. The combination of these two trends would cause the R value to reduce over time for a given application. Software application efficiency improvements, compiler optimization improvements, and increasing sizes of datasets (in relation to the size of available cache layers used in accessing the data) can increase the R value associated with a given workload.

SCPM Load Planning

For a simplified example of a server with an SCPM value of 40,000, the following measurements were taken for a steady state of 300 users and 50 transactions per second during the peak measured shift:

Average CPU Utilization	75%
Average Disk Reads per Second	3000
Average Disk Writes per Second	1500
Total Disk Avtivities per Second	4500
Filesystem I/O Size	8KB

Using these measurements and assuming that transactions are flowing at a relatively constant rate, we can characterize the workload in many interesting ways, as shown in the following projection examples:

QC	(40,000 (Q))	* (.75)	30,000 Q
QC / User	(30,000 (Q))	/ (300 (Users))	100 Q
QC / Transaction	(30,000 (Q))	/ (50 (Transactions))	600 Q*sec
S_W / User	(1500 (writes))	/ (300 (Users))	5 IOPS
S_R / User	(3000 (reads))	/ (300 (Users))	10 IOPS
S / User	(4500 (I/Os))	/ (300 (Users))	15 IOPS
S_W / Transaction	(1500 (writes))	/ (50 (Transactions))	30 IOPS
S_R / Transaction	(3000 (reads))	/ (50 (Transactions))	60 IOPS
S / Transaction	(4500 (I/Os))	/ (50 (Transactions))	90 IOPS
T_{Disk}	(4500 (I/Os))	* (8 (KB))	36 MB/sec

During our monthly load planning meeting, the marketing department presented a growth projection of 50% for the next fiscal quarter, causing the business unit consuming the service to increase their transactional and user community volumes by 50% to meet the demands.

QC	(30,000 (QC)) * (1.5)	45,000 Q
S_W	(1500 (writes)) * (1.5)	2250 IOPS
S_R	(3000 (reads)) * (1.5)	4500 IOPS
S	(4500 (I/Os)) * (1.5)	6750 IOPS
T_{Disk}	3.6 MB/sec * (1.5)	5.4 MB/sec

We can now apply these projections against our system's capabilities to predict the system utilization while running the new workload volumes. The server running the workload has an SCPM value of 40,000 Q, and the load projection shows a processing requirement of 45,000 Q. From these values, it is obvious that the current server will not be able to process the projected workload. If we upgrade the server through module count increases, CPU module upgrades, or a "forklift upgrade" to an entirely new machine with an SCPM value of 72,000 Q, we can predict the utilization of the server running the projected workload. The optimal case would allow us to run the current measured workload of user and transactional volumes on the new server system to validate our workload model, but this is rarely the case in a rapid growth environment. The following formula predicts the system utilization while the new workload volumes are running:

System Utilization = QC ÷ SCPM (Q)

45,000 ÷ 72,000 = 62.5%

Similarly, the projected disk utilization can be predicted based on the capabilities of the disk subsystem (in throughput and IOPS), and the projected throughput consumption and generated IOPS of the workload after applying the growth introduced in the load planning process.

Workload Characterization

In cases where the workload is defined but not measurable (for example, for a new system under development), historical data can be used from past measured systems to characterize a likely resource consumption with a reasonable rate of accuracy. In our applications of this process and from studies of both internal and external customer data, we were able to identify and characterize very predictable system performance characteristics based on generic definitions of workload type. Regardless of the actual application, OLTP servers generally consume disk, CPU, and memory resources at a similar rate.

By applying the SCPM process, some historical rules of thumb for hardware peripheral behavior, and basic measurement and application of Amdahl's law for th measured workload, we can generate reasonably accurate system capacity models for a known workload. The SCPM process has proved very effective in modelling and predicting workloads and resource consumption for a large percentage of the machines sampled. Some workloads do break the mold, and are not as predictable a the vast majority.

In some cases, applications will consume some critical resources or cause contention for which the SCPM process cannot predict. These fringe cases must be accounted for using more accurate and intensive (and thus more expensive) methods in addition to the SCPM process, where very accurate models are critical. These intensive capacity, performance measurement, and prediction methods include:

- Discrete event modelling
- Benchmarks
- Simulation
- Queuing theory application
- Finite resource consumption studies

The SCPM process is very useful in a first pass of a TCO analysis as part of a server consolidation effort. Estimated machine and workload characteristics can be computed and predictions can be made against a computing environment to suppor the current and future computing needs of the enterprise.

Capacity Planning for Complex Disk Subsystems

The details of how disk measurements are derived are covered in-depth by Adrian Cockcroft in *Sun Performance and Tuning* and the Sun BluePrints book *Resource Management*. Brian Wong, in his book *Configuration and Capacity Planning for Solaris Servers*, describes the architecture and performance characteristics of disk subsystems based on SCSI and Fibre Channel. Here we focus on extending the use of conventional `iostat`-based data to take into account the configuration of a more complex disk subsystem.

Disk response time is slow at nearly 100% busy, but a striped volume or hardware RAID unit still seems to respond quickly at high utilization levels. This occurs because more complex systems do not follow the same rules as simple systems when it comes to response time, throughput, and utilization. Even the simple systems are not so simple, so we start by looking at measurements available for a single disk, then observe combinations, and finally show you how to combine the available measurements into capacity estimates.

Capacity Measurements for Single Disks

Single disks are quite simple to plan for, and their performance characteristics can usually be obtained from the disk vendor's Web site. The essential characteristics for each disk are its average seek time (which may be different for reads and writes), its average formatted transfer rate, and its spindle speed in RPM. For example, a high-end server 18.2 GB FC-AL drive is the Seagate ST318203FC, with 5.2 ms read seek, 6.0 ms write seek, 24.5 MB/s transfer rate, and 10,000 RPM.

The most important measurement to take on each disk is the average transfer size. This may be very stable or it may fluctuate depending on the workload. In some cases, you may need to break down the day into shifts or modes (e.g., online mode, backup mode) and analyze capacity for each mode separately.

Measurements on a Single Disk

The device driver maintains a queue of waiting requests, which are serviced one at a time by the disk. The terms *utilization, service time, wait time, throughput,* and *wait queue length* have well-defined meanings in this scenario, and for a single disk, this setup (FIGURE 5-11) is so simple that a very basic queuing model fits it well.

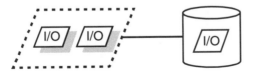

FIGURE 5-11 Simple Disk Model

Over time, disk technology has moved on. These days, a standard disk is SCSI-based and has an embedded controller. The disk drive contains a small microprocessor and about 1 MB of RAM. It can typically handle up to 64 outstanding requests via SCSI tagged-command queuing. The system uses a SCSI host bus adapter (HBA) to talk to the disk. Large systems have another level of intelligence and buffering in a hardware RAID controller. The simple model of a disk used by iostat and its terminology have become confused. In addition, the same reporting mechanism is used for client-side NFS mount points and complex disk volumes set up by Solstice DiskSuite™ software or Veritas Volume Manager (VxVM).

In the old days, if the device driver sent a request to the disk, the disk would do nothing else until it completed the request. The time it took was the service time, and the average service time was a property of the disk itself. Disks that spin faster and seek faster have lower (better) service times. With today's systems, if the device driver issues a request, that request is queued internally by the RAID controller and the disk drive and several more requests can be sent before the first one comes back. The service time, as measured by the device driver, varies according to the load level and queue length, and is not directly comparable to the old-style service time of a simple disk drive. The response time is defined as the total waiting time in the queue plus the service time. Unfortunately, `iostat` reports response time but labels it `svc_t`. We'll see later how to calculate the actual service time for a simple disk.

Consider the utilization of the device. As soon as the device has one request in its internal queue, it becomes busy, and the proportion of the time that it is busy is the utilization. If there is always a request waiting, the device is 100% busy. Since a single disk only completes one I/O request at a time, it saturates at 100% busy. If the device has a large number of requests and is intelligent enough to reorder them, it may reduce the average service time and increase the throughput as more load is applied, even though it is already at 100% utilization.

FIGURE 5-12 shows how a busy disk can operate more efficiently than a lightly loaded disk. The difference is that the service time is lower for the busy disk, but the response time is longer. This difference is because all the requests are present in the queue at the start, so the response time for the last request includes waiting for every other request to complete. In the lightly loaded case, each request is serviced as it is made, so there is no waiting and response time is the same as the service time. When you hear your disk rattling on a desktop system as you start an application, it is because the head is seeking back and forth, as shown in the first example below of disk activity not taking advantage of I/O request queuing. Unfortunately, starting an application tends to generate a single thread of page-in disk reads and until one is completed, the next one is not issued; so, you end up with a fairly busy disk with only one request in the queue and it cannot be optimized. If the disk is on a busy server instead, lots of accesses are coming in parallel from different transactions and different users, so you will get a full queue and more efficient disk usage overall.

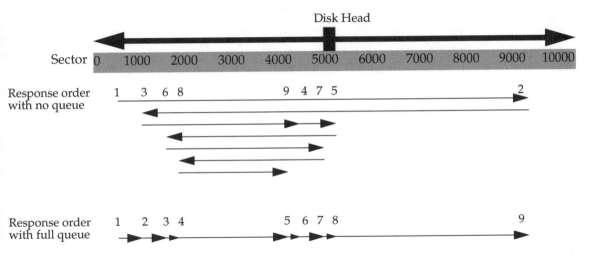

FIGURE 5-12 Disk Head Movements for a Request Sequence

Solaris OE Disk Instrumentation

The instrumentation provided in the Solaris OE accounts for this change by explicitly measuring a two-stage queue: one queue, called the wait queue, in the device driver, and another queue, called the active queue, in the device itself. A read or write command is issued to the device driver and sits in the wait queue until the SCSI bus and disk are both ready. When the command is sent to the disk device, it moves to the active queue until the disk sends its response. FIGURE 5-13 shows example `iostat -x` output for a single disk in the common format supported in all Solaris 2 OE releases.

```
% iostat -x
                                 extended device statistics
device    r/s  w/s    kr/s    kw/s wait actv   svc_t   %w   %b
sd106     0.0  0.0     0.0     0.0  0.0  0.0     0.0    0    0
```

FIGURE 5-13 Example `iostat -x` Output

FIGURE 5-14 shows the output of `iostat -xn`, which separates `svc_t` into its two subcomponents and gives a more useful name to the device. This format was introduced in Solaris 2.6 OE, and at the same time, disk slices, tapes, and NFS mount points were added to the underlying kernel data source.

```
% iostat -xn
                                 extended device statistics
   r/s  w/s    kr/s    kw/s wait actv wsvc_t asvc_t   %w   %b device
  21.9 63.5 1159.1 2662.9  0.0  2.7    0.0   31.8    0   93 c3t15d0
```

FIGURE 5-14 Example `iostat -xn` Output

The problem with `iostat` is that it tries to report the new measurements in some of the original terminology. The "wait service time" is actually the time spent in the "wait" queue. This is not the right definition of service time in any case, and the word *wait* is being used to mean two different things (see FIGURE 5-15).

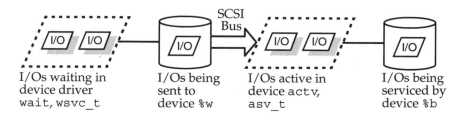

FIGURE 5-15 Two-Stage Disk Model Used by Solaris 2 OE

Utilization (U) is defined to be the busy time (B) as a percentage of the total time (T), as shown in the following examples:

$$U_{wait} = \text{Wait Queue Utilization} = \texttt{iostat \%w} = \frac{100 \times B_{wait}}{T_{hires}}$$

$$U_{run} = \text{Run Queue Utilization} = \texttt{iostat \%b} = \frac{100 \times B_{run}}{T_{hires}}$$

Now, we get to something called service time (S), but it is *not* what `iostat` prints out and calls service time. This is the real thing! The following examples demonstrate that it can be calculated as the busy time (B) divided by the number of accesses that completed, or alternately, as the utilization (U) divided by the throughput (X):

$$S_{wait} = \text{Average Wait Queue Service Time in Milliseconds} = \frac{B_{wait}}{C \times 100000} = \frac{U_{wait}}{X}$$

$$S_{run} = \text{Average Run Queue Service Time in Milliseconds} = \frac{B_{run}}{C \times 100000} = \frac{U_{run}}{X}$$

The meaning of S_{run} is as close as you can get to the old-style disk service time. Remember that modern disks can queue more than one command at a time and can return them in a different order than they were issued, and it becomes clear that it cannot be the same thing. To calculate it from `iostat` output, divide the utilization by the total number of reads and writes as shown from the values in the following example:

```
% iostat -xn
   r/s  w/s    kr/s    kw/s wait actv wsvc_t asvc_t  %w  %b device
  21.9 63.5 1159.1 2662.9  0.0  2.7    0.0   31.8   0  93 c3t15d0
```

In this case, U = 93% (0.93) and throughput $X = \texttt{r/s} + \texttt{w/s} = 21.9 + 63.5 = 85.4$. So, service time $S = U/X = 0.011 = 11$ ms, and the reported response time $R = 31.8$ ms. The queue length is reported as 2.7; this makes sense, since each request has to wait in the queue for several other requests to be serviced.

With the SE Toolkit, a modified version of iostat written in SE prints out the response time and the service time data using the format shown in FIGURE 5-16.

```
% se siostat.se 10
03:42:50  ------throughput------ -----wait queue----- ----active queue----
disk      r/s  w/s  Kr/s  Kw/s qlen res_t svc_t %ut qlen res_t svc_t %ut
c0t2d0s0  0.0  0.2   0.0   1.2 0.00  0.02  0.02   0 0.00 22.87 22.87   0
03:43:00  ------throughput------ -----wait queue----- ----active queue----
disk      r/s  w/s  Kr/s  Kw/s qlen res_t svc_t %ut qlen res_t svc_t %ut
c0t2d0s0  0.0  3.2   0.0  23.1 0.00  0.01  0.01   0 0.72 225.45 16.20   5
```

FIGURE 5-16 SE-Based Rewrite of iostat to Show Service Time Correctly

We can get the number that iostat calls service time. It is defined as the queue length (Q, shown by iostat with the headings "wait" and "actv") divided by the throughput, but it is actually the residence or response time and includes all queuing effects, as shown in the following examples:

$$R_{wait} = \text{Average Wait Queue Response Time} = \texttt{iostat} \quad \texttt{wsvc\_t} = \frac{Q_{wait}}{X}$$

$$R_{run} = \text{Average Run Queue Response Time} = \texttt{iostat} \ \texttt{asvc\_t} = \frac{Q_{run}}{X}$$

Taking the values from our iostat example, $R = Q \div X = 2.7 \div 85.4 = 0.0316 = 31.6$ ms, which is nearly the same as what iostat reports. The difference is 31.6 vs. 31.8 and is due to rounding errors in the reported values, 2.7 and 85.4. With full precision, the result is identical, since this is how iostat calculates the response time.

Another way to express response time is in terms of service time and utilization. This method uses a theoretical model of response time, which assumes that as you approach 100% utilization with a constant service time, the response time increases to infinity, as shown below:

$$R_{wait} = \text{Average Wait Queue Response Time Prediction} = \texttt{iostat} \quad \texttt{wsvc\_t} = \frac{S_{wait}}{1 - U_{wait}}$$

$$R_{run} = \text{Average Run Queue Response Time Prediction} = \texttt{iostat asvc\_t} = \frac{S_{run}}{1 - U_{run}}$$

Take our example again: $R = S \div (1 - U) = 0.011 \div (1 - 0.93) = 0.157 = 157$ ms. This is a lot more than the measured response time of 31.8 ms, so the disk is operating better than the simple model predicts for high utilizations. This occurs because the disk is much more complex than the model and is actively trying to optimize itself; the service time is not constant, and the incoming data is not as random as the model. However, the model does provide the right characteristic and can be used as a simple way to do a worst-case analysis.

Complex Resource Utilization Characteristics

One important characteristic of complex I/O subsystems is that the utilization measurement can be confusing. When a simple system reaches 100% busy, it has also reached its maximum throughput because only one thing is being processed at a time in the I/O device. When the device being monitored is an NFS server, hardware RAID disk subsystem, or striped volume, the situation is clearly much more complex. All of these can process many requests in parallel. A simple view of this complexity that approximates the results reported by `iostat` for a Solstice DiskSuite MetaDisk stripe is shown in FIGURE 5-17. The VxVM acts the same way, but does not report any data via `iostat`.[1]

---

1. Veritas Corp. does not support the Solaris OE disk `kstat` information, but Veritas Corp. does report a subset of this information via the `vxstat` utility. Veritas Corp. does not publish a programming interface that is readable by `iostat` -like tools.

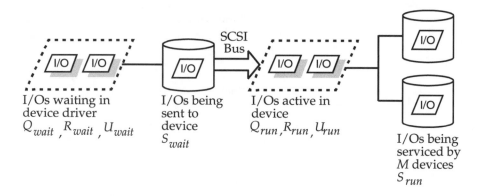

FIGURE 5-17 Complex I/O Device Queue Model

As long as a single I/O is being serviced at all times, the utilization is reported by iostat as 100%, which makes sense because it means that the pool of devices is always busy doing something. However, there is enough capacity for additional I/Os to be serviced in parallel. Compared to a simple device, the service time for each I/O is the same, but the queue is being drained more quickly, so the average queue length and response time is less and the peak throughput is more. In effect, the load on each disk is divided by the number of disks, so the true utilization of the striped disk volume is actually below 100%. The true utilization must be divided across the number of devices, M. The average utilization of the underlying drives is much lower than iostat reports. The combined throughput and service time is normally called the service intensity rho, and it is like a utilization that can be over 100%.

An alternative approach to this issue argues that if several requests can be serviced at once, then when a queuing model is used, the model works as if the average service time was reduced by the same factor, and utilization is still only up to 100%.

So, there is some confusion here over how to handle this case. Either the service time or the utilization must be divided by the number of underlying disks. Each of these two cases is, in fact, valid in different situations.

For the first case, we assume that each disk I/O request is small, that it cannot be further subdivided, and that it will access a single disk. This is normally the case when the request size is smaller than the stripe interlace. Each request picks a disk at random, then provides the usual service time, so overall, the utilization of all the disks is reduced by the factor M.

For the second case, we assume that each disk request is large—ideally, a full-stripe access, which is subdivided into many smaller requests that hit the entire set of disks. In this case, all the disks are kept busy, so the utilization of each individual disk is the same as the utilization of the entire set. However, the service time for each of the small requests is less than the service time of the big one, so we see a reduced service time.

Cached Disk Subsystem Optimizations

When a cache is introduced, a certain proportion of the accesses will hit the cache, but it is not often possible to obtain a measurement of this proportion. The cache also allows many optimizations that combine small accesses into fewer larger accesses to take place. Some of the common optimizations are:

- *Read prefetch clustering* – A small read triggers a larger read into cache, then subsequent nearby reads and writes are satisfied by the cache. Modified cache blocks are written back asynchronously. The service time of the first read will be increased somewhat, and the service time of subsequent read and write hits will be very quick. A write-back may cause a delay to subsequent accesses.

- *Asynchronous write caching* – If the cache is nonvolatile, it is safe to acknowledge the write immediately and to write the data to disk later on. The service time of the write will always be fast as long as a cache block is available. Write-backs can become a bottleneck and cause cache block allocation delays that slow down write service times.

- *Write cancellation* – Multiple writes to the same block often occur when file system metadata is updating. When the block is cached, subsequent writes cancel out the first one and many updates can occur for each write-back to disk.

- *Write coalescing* – Multiple writes to adjacent data are coalesced into a single larger write. If the larger write exceeds the underlying disk block size, then there is no need to read a large block because it modifies it by incorporating the small write and writes the large block back.

All of these optimizations can be happening at the same time, and there is no standard way for the disk subsystem to report what is going on in its cache. In most cases, the disk and cache do not collect this kind of information at all. In the next section, to make sense of the data reported by iostat, we need some configuration information, a simplified model of the cached disk subsystem, and some assumptions about the workload mix.

Cached Disk Subsystems

There is a lot of read caching being done by the file system in main memory, but the file system cannot do write caching safely for logs, metadata, or database transactions, and this is where performance bottlenecks often occur.

The disk cache can be inserted into the disk subsystem in two places: in the host computer or in the disk array. The Sun Prestoserve and Sun StorEdge™ Fast Write Cache products add nonvolatile memory to the host computer and use it primarily as a write cache. A very small amount of read-back from the cache may occur, but usually the source data is still available to be read from main memory longer than it is stored in cache. To simplify the model, we can assume that reads always go to the underlying disks and writes always go to the write cache first. The capacity model for reads is the same as that of a simple striped disk setup; read prefetch optimizations are done by the file system layer in both cases, so for raw disk, there is no prefetch or read cache in either case.

The model for writes is that writes are extremely fast until the write cache is overwhelmed. This overwhelming occurs when the underlying disks cannot cope with the rate at which data is being flushed from the cache. The slight CPU overhead from the extra copying of the data can be estimated from the maximum access rate of the NVRAM. The worst-case performance for writes is limited by the write-back rate and is about the same as for an uncached system. There can be a choice of policies for the cache: it might cache only synchronous writes, or it could cache all writes. It is best to cache all writes to start with; also, if the write-backs saturate, drop back to only caching synchronous writes.

Host-Based Write Cache Model Interconnect Parameters

UltraSCSI runs at close to 40 MB/s for large transfers, but reads and writes compete on the same bus. This interconnect is used for simple disk packs and the Sun D1000 and A1000. The A3500 uses dual load-balanced UltraSCSI buses for a total of almost 80 MB/s. The transfer latency for small transfers over UltraSCSI is around 0.6 ms.

Fibre Channel has the advantage that reads and writes use separate paths. The Fibre Channel Arbitrated Loop (FC-AL) standard can suffer from arbitration delays when very long loops are used, but small configurations are much faster than UltraSCSI. The older SPARCStorage™ Array (SSA) runs at 25 MB/s in each direction, and at about 1.0 ms minimum transfer latency. The current FC-AL standard runs at up to 100 MB/s each way, with latency of about 0.4 ms.

Dual FC-AL loops have been measured at up to 180 MB/s, again with a latency of about 0.4 ms. If both loops run over the same SBus interface, the SBus itself may become a bottleneck.

Estimating Capacity for Complex Disk Subsystems

This section provides an overview of performance factors and capacity planning models for complex disk subsystems. It includes RAID5 and cached stripe examples.

Single Disks

The capacity model for a single disk is simple and has already been described. The schematic in FIGURE 5-18 shows a single disk with incoming and outgoing requests. In the following sections, we extend the schematic to show more complex disk configurations.

FIGURE 5-18 Single Disk Schematic

Mirrored Disks

FIGURE 5-19 is an example of mirrored disks.

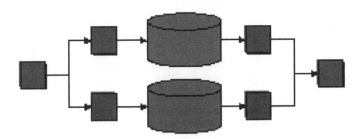

FIGURE 5-19 Mirrored Disks Schematic

All writes go to both disks when they are mirrored. However, there are several read policy alternatives, such as:

- All reads from one side (referred to as "preferred")

- Alternate from side to side (referred to as "round-robin")
- Split by block number to reduce seek
- Read both, and use first to respond

We can make a simple capacity assumption if we assume that duplicated interconnects are configured. Overall, the capacity of a mirrored pair of disks or volumes is the same as the capacity unmirrored. In practice, writes take a small hit and reads a small benefit, but these are second-order effects that can be ignored for the sake of simplicity.

Concatenated and Fat Stripe Disks

FIGURE 5-20 illustrates concatenated and fat stripe disks.

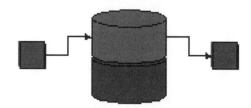

FIGURE 5-20 Concatenated and Fat Stripe Disks Schematic

When disks are concatenated or the request size is less than the interlace, individual requests will only go to one disk. If the workload consists of single-threaded requests, then you will only have the same capacity as a single disk, regardless of how many disks there are in the stripe. Single-threaded accesses are typical for log disks.

Multithreaded requests can make good use of this disk configuration, as long as the requests are evenly distributed over concatenated disks or the stripe size is not too large. This is a common situation for database tables where small requests of 2 to 8 kilobytes are used and it is impractical to attempt to make a stripe interlace this small.

This configuration has the same service time as one disk, since any one request always hits a single disk. It has the throughput of N disks if more than N threads are evenly distributed.

Striped Disk Accesses

FIGURE 5-21 illustrates striped disk accesses.

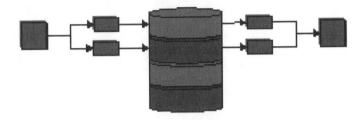

FIGURE 5-21 Striped Disk Accesses Schematic

When the request size is more than the interlace size, it will be split over N disks for both single- and multithreaded requests. N is set by the request size divided by the interlace. The throughput of N disks is obtained.

The reduced size of the request on each underlying stripe reduces service time for large transfers, but you need to wait for all disks to complete, and the slowest dominates. This kind of operation works efficiently when one-megabyte requests are split into a 128 K interlace. As the request size and interlace are reduced, the overall efficiency also reduces.

RAID5 for Small Requests

FIGURE 5-22 illustrates RAID5 for small requests.

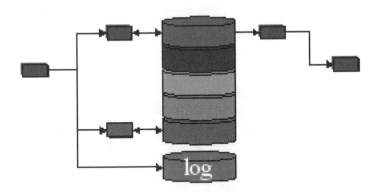

FIGURE 5-22 RAID5 for Small Requests Schematic

The operation of RAID5 is described in detail in *Configuration and Capacity Planning for Sun Servers* by Brian Wong. In essence, a parity disk is maintained alongside a stripe to provide storage that is protected against failure, without the full duplication overhead of mirroring. Writes must calculate parity that is rotated through the disks. A write must do the following:

1. Read the parity and old data blocks.

2. Insert the small write into the block.

3. Calculate new parity data.

4. Write to a separate log that ensures consistent data integrity.

5. Write data and parity back to the disk.

The problem is that this sequence takes approximately triple the service time of a normal write and one-third the throughput of a single disk. This situation may be encountered with software RAID5 implementations of DiskSuite and VxVM when the workload consists of many small writes.

Reading the RAID5 combination performs like a normal stripe, with a throughput of N-1 disks and service time of one.

If a disk has failed, the read must reconstruct the missing data by performing extra reads; overall, it is best to assume that degraded mode throughput is about the same as one disk.

RAID5 for Large Requests

FIGURE 5-23 illustrates RAID5 for large requests.

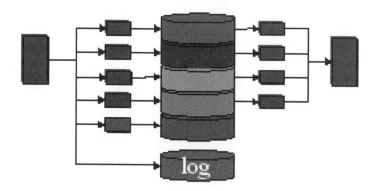

FIGURE 5-23 RAID5 for Large Requests Schematic

When a write is large enough to include the full stripe width, there is no need to read any of the data, so all the writes and the parity can be written immediately. Capacity is similar to a stripe; it has similar read and write performance and the throughput of N-1 disks. The service time for the transfer is reduced as the size of each write is reduced by the factor N-1.

Overall, there is less load on the disk interconnect than it takes to keep a mirror synchronized.

If a disk fails in degraded mode, throughput and service are similar since the entire stripe is read and written as a unit. Extra CPU time is used to regenerate the missing data.

Cached RAID5

FIGURE 5-24 illustrates cached RAID5.

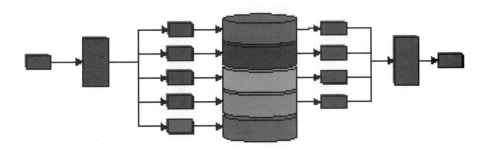

FIGURE 5-24 Cached RAID5 Schematic

When a nonvolatile RAM cache is added to a RAID5 setup, it works much more efficiently. There is no need for a recovery log disk, since the log that keeps track of partially complete operations can be kept in nonvolatile memory.

The cache provides fast service time for all writes. Interconnect transfer time is the only component. The cache optimizes RAID5 operations because it allows all writes, whether large or small, to be converted to the optimal full-stripe operations.

The RAM cache is not normally large enough (in comparison to the size of the disks) to provide any benefit to read performance.

Cached Stripe

FIGURE 5-25 illustrates cached stripe.

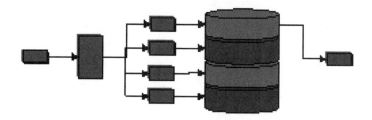

FIGURE 5-25 Cached Stripe Schematic

Write-caching for stripes provides greatly reduced service time. It is worthwhile for small transfers, but large transfers should not be cached.

For the A3500, some tests confirm that 128 K is the crossover point at which the same performance is obtained with and without the cache. For consistently larger transfers, better performance is obtained without a write cache. For smaller transfers, much better performance is obtained with the write cache.

Write caches also perform a few useful optimizations. Rewriting the same block over and over again cancels in the cache so that only one write needs to be made. Small sequential writes also coalesce to form fewer larger writes.

Capacity Model Measurements

Measurements are derived from `iostat` output and knowledge of the configuration of the disk subsystem.

Some example output from `iostat -x` is shown below, with measurements derived from it:

```
extended disk statistics
disk      r/s  w/s   Kr/s   Kw/s wait actv   svc_t  %w   %b
sd9      33.1  8.7  271.4   71.3  0.0  2.3    15.8   0   27
```

- Utilization $U = \%b \div 100 = 0.27$
- Throughput $X = r \div s + w \div s = 41.8$
- Size $K = Kr \div s + Kw \div s \div X = 8.2K$
- Concurrency $N = \texttt{actv} = 2.3$

- Service time $S = U \div X = 6.5$ ms
- Response time $R = \texttt{svc\_t} = 15.8$ ms

The configuration parameters for this system are:

- Number of data disks $M = 4$ (ignore mirrors)
- Do not include RAID5 parity disks
- Stripe interlace $I = 64$K (use whole disk size if unstriped)
- Max SCSI rate $Brw = 40000$K/s or FC-AL $Br = Bw = 100000$K/s
- Max disk data rate $D = 24500$K/s

Disk and Controller Capacity

Here we check for a throughput-based bottleneck; we sum `kr/s` and `kw/s` by controller for all the disks on that controller.

```
% iostat -xn
                          extended device statistics
  r/s   w/s    kr/s     kw/s wait actv wsvc_t asvc_t   %w    %b device
 21.9  63.5  1159.1   2662.9  0.0  2.7    0.0   31.8    0    93 c3t15d0
```

- $Urw = (\Sigma kr + \Sigma kw) \div D$
- $Ur = \Sigma kr \div Br$
- $Uw = \Sigma kw \div Bw$ or $Urw = (\Sigma kr + \Sigma kw) \div Brw$

Performance Factor P

To simplify the comparison of different disk configurations for a specific workload, a workload-specific performance factor can be calculated. The number of underlying disks that contribute to performance varies from 1 to stripe width M, depending upon configuration and workload.

The performance factor P can vary for read and write, but it does not include cache effects. Here is an example of calculating the performance factor P.

For small IOPS $K \leq I$, that is, request (K) is less than interlace (I).

If we assume that requests are aligned with the stripe interlace, then for any request smaller than the interlace, the request will hit only a single disk.

We use the notation of M disks, with a workload concurrency of N.

$P = max(1, min(M, N))$, that is, at least 1, and no more than M or N.

For large IOPS, $K > I$, that is, request (K) is more than interlace (I).

The number of disks involved in each request should always be rounded up to the next integer. If we divide the size by the interlace, as soon as the result is over 1.0, we have to round it up to 2.0 because both disks will be involved. In general, we divide K by I and round the result up to the next whole number. We can use the notation $roundup(K \div I)$ to show this.

There is an effective increase in concurrency at the disk level because each thread of access in the workload is being subdivided by the disk interlace to cause more threads of disk accesses. This division allows more performance to be obtained from a disk subsystem, up to the limit of the number of disks in the stripe.

$P = max(1, min(M, N \times roundup(K \div I)))$

Example 1

You can perform a capacity estimation from `iostat` with the example data shown below and for $M = 6$ disks, $I = 128K$ interlace:

```
 r/s   w/s    kr/s    kw/s wait actv wsvc_t asvc_t   %w    %b device
21.9 63.5 1159.1 2662.9  0.0  2.7    0.0   31.8    0    93 c3t15d0
```

kr = 53K read size, kw = 42K write size, N = 2.7 threads, and $S = 0.93/(21.9 + 63.5) =$ 10.9 ms service time.

Performance is limited by the number of threads to $P = 2.7$. Utilization reported by `iostat` is $U_{iostat} = 0.93$, but the effective utilization of the stripe is divided by P, so $U_{stripe} = U_{iostat} \div P = 0.34$. Therefore, the stripe is 34% busy and has 66% spare capacity for this workload.

Example 2

This example is based on the same `iostat` data shown above, but for $M = 6$ and $I = 16K$ interlace. The change in the interlace would change the data reported by `iostat` in practice, so the results are not comparable with Example 1.

Since the interlace is smaller than the read and write sizes, you can calculate that $roundup(kr \div I) = 4$ and $roundup(kw \div I) = 3$. This is then multiplied by N, the number of threads, and however you calculate it, the full stripe width of six disks will be utilized by this workload, so $P = 6$. The stripe utilization is divided down from

$U_{iostat} \div P = 0.93 \div 6$ to $U_{stripe} = 0.16$. The stripe is 16% busy and has 84% spare capacity for this workload. The average service time is effectively $S = 0.16 \div (21.9 + 63.5) = 1.9$ ms.

Cache Performance Impact Factors

The effect of cache on throughput is hard to model because there is no instrumentation to indicate the occurrence of clustering and write cancellation improvements. There is also a small overhead from copying data to and from the cache on its way to the disk. You should make the pessimistic assumption that throughput is unchanged by the cache.

The primary benefit of cache is fast response time. The benefit can be summarized by two cache efficiency factors: E and H.

E is defined as the service time speed-up due to cache for reads and writes. $E = 1.0$ is the same as uncached. $E = S_{disk} \div S_{cache}$, and we can also assume that $E_{read} = E_{write}$ is a close enough approximation to prevent the need to calculate reads and writes separately.

H is defined as the cache hit rate. $H = 0.0$ for uncached requests, and $H = 1.0$ (i.e., 100%) for fully cached requests. H varies greatly with workload mix and intensity changes. It must be calculated separately for reads and writes, since H_{read} and H_{write} have very different values.

Service Time and Cache Hit Rate

You can infer the cache hit rate from knowing disk and cache service times.

The measured service time calculated from `iostat` data is
$S_{measured} = S_{disk}(1 - H) + H \times S_{disk} \div E$; that is, the slow proportion of cache misses plus the fast proportion of cache hits. We can turn this calculation around, using measurements or estimates of the values of E and S_{disk} to get an estimate of the cache hit rate:

$$H_{estimated} = (1 - S_{measured}/S_{disk}) \div (1 - 1/E)$$

This calculation is sensitive to errors and variations in the values of S_{disk} and E. If the results of the estimate are outside the permissible range of H (0.0 to 1.0), then you need to make sure that S_{disk} is in particular big enough.

S_{disk} must be the worst-possible-case disk service time.

$S_{disk} \div E$ must be the best-possible-case cache hit service time.

Solid-state disks have $H = 1.0$ for both reads and writes as data is engulfed by the cache. Other disk types have varying values for H, but characteristic values for E. Some example cache values are:

- Cached disk array or solid-state disk with UltraSCSI interface, $E \approx 10$; with FC-AL interface, $E \approx 15$
- Sun StorEdge Fast Write Cache product uses mirrored 32 MB NVRAM cards, no read cache, $E \approx 500$
- File system read cache, that is, access to a data file already in memory, no device driver involved, $E \approx 5000$

Main memory provides the best cache for reads, and NVRAM provides the best cache for writes. The only disadvantage of the NVRAM cache is that in clustered, highly available disk subsystems, it cannot be used because it is internal to each system.

Caveats

This discussion has concentrated on first-order effects. Many simplifying assumptions have been made, so do not depend on this model for fine accuracy. You should use this model to get into the right "ballpark," so you can configure your disk subsystem appropriately for your workload.

Summary

This chapter focused on CPU, memory, disk capacity estimation, and the varying scalability characteristics that create complicated disk subsystems. In addition, this chapter gave examples of system resource modelling and also looked at some of the problems of capacity planning for CPU and disk subsystems.

The next chapter concentrates on the importance of observability requirements for information collection and presentation to three different audiences.

CHAPTER 6

Observability

Observability is the first requirement for performance management and capacity planning. The performance characteristics need to be presented in a way that makes sense to those who are looking at them, so they can observe the behavior of the systems and understand what is happening. Three different viewpoints need to be provided for different audiences:

- Operations
- Management
- Engineering

Each audience requires significantly different information. This information can be obtained from disparate output of the same performance database or with completely separate tools. This chapter looks in detail at gathering, organizing, and presenting system performance data to these three audiences.

Operations Viewpoint

The operations room works in the immediate time frame, using a real-time display, updated every few seconds. Alert-based monitoring should be combined with automatic high-level problem diagnosis if possible. However, this level of sophistication is rare. Simple high-level graphs and views of current data will be needed.

Management Viewpoint

Management will never have time to read a voluminous report. A single-page daily summary of status and problems is more appropriate. The summary should contain:

- Business-oriented metrics
- Future scenario planning
- Concise report with dashboard-style status indicators

Marketing and management input is needed to define the scenarios. These form a grid, with things that change the load level down the side and things that change the capacity across the top. It is then easy to see which tuning and upgrade projects must be implemented to cope with the increased load of the next marketing campaign.

Engineering Viewpoint

Engineers need to see large volumes of detailed data at several different time scales. The data is used as input to tuning, reconfiguring, and developing future products, and aids in low-level problem diagnosis.

You only need to generate and store large volumes of raw data on systems that are being tuned. Detailed reports with drill-down and correlation analysis are needed, and many tools implement this kind of functionality very well. Engineers know how to build tools, and they tend to build the tools that they need themselves, so good engineering-oriented features are common.

Example Scenarios

In the following sections, techniques and examples for implementing these viewpoints are presented. The operations viewpoint is demonstrated with the Sun Management Center (SunMC, a.k.a. Sun Enterprise SyMON™ 2.1). The engineering viewpoint is implemented with SunMC and the SE toolkit to collect additional detailed data. The management viewpoint is implemented as a spreadsheet.

Operations Viewpoint Implementation

This section describes an implementation of operations management that is generic in the techniques being used, but specific in the tools used to implement it in a primarily Sun based environment.

The steps covered in this section illustrate how to use a system monitor to automate the process of tracking multiple systems for unusual or problematic conditions.

1. **Enable rules.**

   Many monitoring tools are shipped with their monitoring capability unconfigured or partially enabled, so the first step is to enable all relevant rules. If you have BMC Patrol (www.bmc.com), load Knowledge Modules. With SunMC, basic rules are enabled, but you can load additional health monitoring tools.

2. Set up rule thresholds.

The default rules may be set up for a small system, in which case, they can generate false alarms on a much larger server. They may also be set too high, so a problem could occur without firing the alarm. For all the rules that you have, you should make a list of each rule, listing its threshold values and the typical and maximum metric values you see in normal operation. If you can identify the values for these metrics seen during problem situations, then you can set alert thresholds correctly to indicate transitions from normal (green) to high (yellow) to problematic (red) levels. If you have never seen a problem with a particular metric, then set its threshold a little higher than the highest value you have ever seen. This way, you "surround" the systems being monitored with a multidimensional behavior envelope. If the behavior goes beyond that envelope in any dimension, then an alarm tells you that something abnormal is happening. Document and save the customized rules and thresholds so they can be replicated on similar systems and are not lost during system upgrades.

3. Monitor and reset alarms.

When an alarm condition occurs, the alarm is useless if no one notices or responds. Usually, the monitoring software will signal that a problem state has occurred, and you can acknowledge the alarm and investigate the source of the problem. Alarms that don't appear to be useful can be disabled, and new alarms can be created to watch metrics that are more relevant to your workload. The alarm log should be archived. The number of alarms that occur at each of the problematic levels (e.g., yellow and red) should be collected daily so it can be reported to management and plotted as a trend over time.

4. Classify problems.

Classify downtime, alarms, and problems that occur which do not cause an alarm in one of the following categories, and report the number of occurrences per day:

- Problem with no corresponding alarm
- Planned downtime
- Planned downtime overrun
- System failure downtime
- Alarm
- Warning
- Persistent known problem carried over from previous day

5. Perform root cause analysis.

For each problem that was counted in Step 4, try to track down the cause and record what you find. If the number of problems analyzed each day matches the number of problems reported, then you are keeping on top of the situation very well. Try to find time to modify the alarm rules to reduce the number of false alarms, warnings, and problems that did not cause a corresponding alarm, such as:

- False alarms
- False warnings
- Alarm rule modifications, for example, to prevent false alarms
- Root cause identifications
- Root cause fixed notifications
- No trouble found notifications

Summarize the problem and analysis counts and types into a daily management report.

Implementing with Sun Management Center

SunMC is used in this example because it is becoming increasingly important as a primary platform for the management and monitoring of Sun systems. Many third-party tools could be used in this role. The primary advantage of these third-party tools is also their primary disadvantage. They are not Sun specific and can manage many kinds of systems from several vendors. But because they are not Sun specific, they do not provide anything comparable to the detailed, platform-specific, active management and diagnosis capabilities of SunMC. The following list summarizes the options and capabilities of SunMC:

- SunMC has third-party vendor support for managing Windows NT-based systems, and relational databases for performing generic system administration functions. Contact Halcyon Inc. (www.halcyon.com) for more details.

- Interoperation with CA Unicenter, BMC Patrol, and HP IT Operations (among others) allows SunMC to integrate into existing multivendor environments.

- The recent addition of a software development kit (SDK) allows anyone to develop extended agent modules and user interface components.

- SunMC is secure, using public key authentication by default, and allows full encryption as a higher overhead option. This feature allows a remote administrator to modify the system configuration safely. Administrative role definitions and access control lists provide flexible security control.

- Full system configuration information is available through SunMC. This capability is not at all trivial to implement, but no other tool can provide anything comparable. Both logical and physical views using pictures of components are available. A recent addition is support for display and management of the Sun Enterprise 10000 servers System Service Processor (SSP) and Dynamic System Domains.

- Hardware products and software to manage the hardware are developed in parallel at Sun; many new hardware and software products will use SunMC as their primary management console or be launched from SunMC.

- Diagnostic tools such as Sun's Configuration Service Tracker (CST) use SunMC as their user interface console.

- Since SunMC is based on the SNMP protocol, it can integrate closely with network management products and tools as a peer, rather than just forwarding SNMP traps. SunMC's SNMP version 2 with user security implementation is more efficient at bulk transfer of data and adds security to the common SNMP standard.

Alert Monitoring with SunMC

SunMC can be used to monitor systems using complex rule-based alerts to diagnose problems. In this section, screenshots illustrate how to configure and use SunMC to perform basic monitoring operations that are useful for operations management. The screenshots in these examples are taken from SunMC 2.1.1, which is a minor update to Sun Enterprise SyMON 2.0 software with a new name and more features.

The SunMC Health Monitor

SunMC includes a system health monitoring module that can be used by operations to simply see if a system has enough resources to run comfortably. For example, if CPU state is reported as *red*, then either less work or more CPU power may be needed on that system. Similarly, if a memory rule reports *red*, then the system may need more memory.

The SunMC health monitor is based on a set of complex rule objects. The health monitor is not enabled by default when SunMC is first installed because only the basic modules are loaded into the agent. The health monitor rules are based on those implemented by Adrian Cockcroft in the SE Toolkit script `virtual_adrian.se` and described by him in *Sun Performance and Tuning: Java and the Internet*.

A simple rule can be placed on any single SunMC metric to monitor its value. Additional rule objects implement more complex rules that refer to several metrics or perform advanced processing on the data.

To load the health monitor module, start SunMC with the default administrative domain, select the system, pop up a menu, then select the Load Module option from the menu, as shown in FIGURE 6-1.

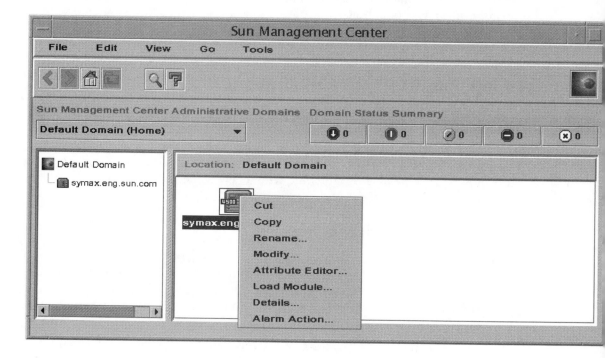

FIGURE 6-1   SunMC Console

Next, scroll down and choose the Health Monitor module; it may already be loaded if SunMC has been preconfigured. Otherwise, select it and click the OK button (see FIGURE 6-2).

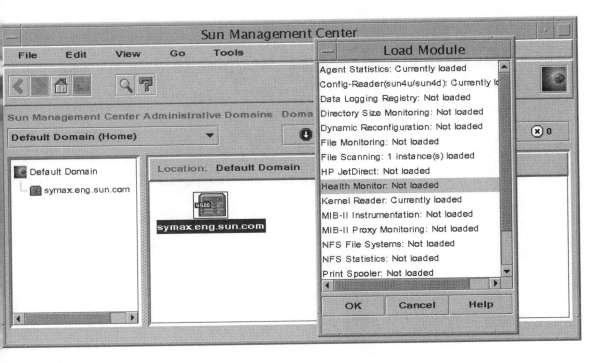

FIGURE 6-2 Load Health Monitor Module

Now, any health monitor alerts will be logged for this system. You could drill down to the subsystem that caused an alert, but we don't expect any health monitor alerts yet, and there is already an unrelated disk space alert on this system. So instead, select the system and open the detailed view. The Details menu option was seen previously when we opened the Load Module window. When it is selected, a second window opens that is specific to the system being monitored (see FIGURE 6-3).

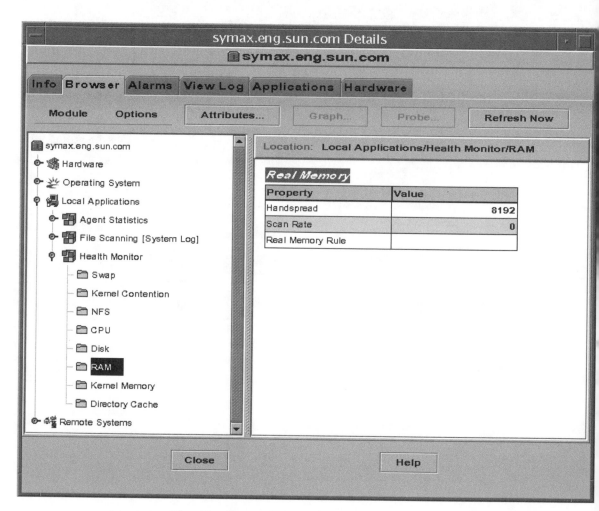

FIGURE 6-3 Host Details Window

The Browser tab of the host Details window shows the modules that are loaded. Under Local Applications (which opens if you click the bullet next to it), you will find the Health Monitor module, and inside that you find the eight rules that are implemented to monitor several system components. Each rule shows a few variables; the RAM rule that is displayed in FIGURE 6-3 shows that the current scan rate is zero, so the rule value is a white box. This box would go red, and the red state would propagate up the hierarchy if the ratio of scan rate to handspread went too high and the page residence time dropped below the preset threshold.

You can view and edit rule attributes and thresholds by popping up a menu over a rule value. The way to use these rules is to increase the thresholds until there are no warnings in normal use on a system that is performing well; then, as the load increases over time, you will start to get warnings that report which subsystem is likely to be the bottleneck. If you have a system that is not performing well to start with, then these rules should help you eliminate some problem areas and suggest which subsystems to concentrate on.

The browser mode can be used to explore all the operating system measurements supplied by the kernel reader for this system, including CPU usage, paging rates, and disk utilization.

Handling Alarms in SunMC

SunMC can monitor hundreds of systems from a single console. Systems can be grouped into various hierarchies; for example, by subnet, application, or department. SunMC gives each group a "cloud" icon; or, you can load a background image to form a map or building plan and then position the icons on the map. When a problem occurs, the status propagates up the hierarchy, causing the clouds to change to the appropriate color, so you can drill down to an individual system. The SunMC console supports multiple administrative domains that can be used by different types of users to see different views of the systems being monitored.

When a simple rule or one of the health monitoring rules generates an alarm, it is logged by SunMC. At the domain-level console, the worst alarm state for each system being monitored is counted. This means that with only one system being monitored, only one alarm will be indicated. In our example, it is in the yellow state.

If you click the yellow indicator, shown in FIGURE 6-4 with a '1' next to it, a new window opens that shows all the alarms for all the systems in this domain.

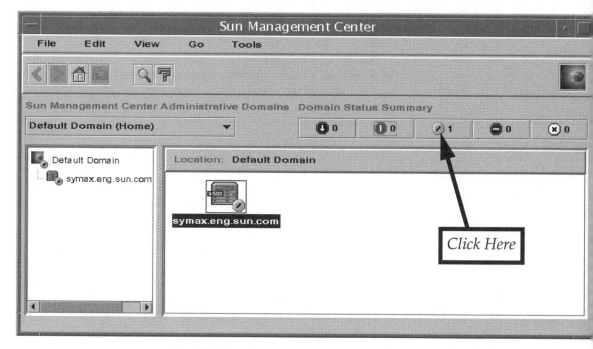

FIGURE 6-4 SunMC Console

FIGURE 6-5 displays only the systems or other network components that are in the yellow (warning) state. In this case, we can see that available swap space is beginning to get low. This very useful form of filtering allows you to handle a flood of alarms from a large number of systems by selecting a domain and dealing with the critical problems for all systems in that domain first.

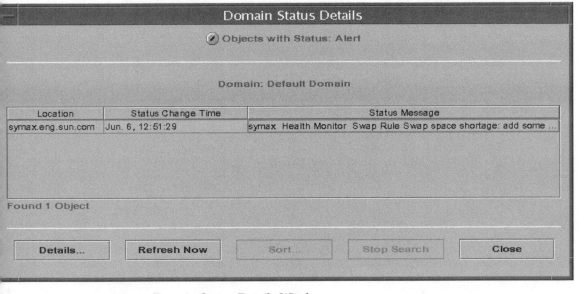

FIGURE 6-5   Domain Status Details Window

If you now either double-click the alarm or select the alarm and click the Details...
button, the Details window for that system opens with its Alarms tab selected, as
shown in FIGURE 6-6.

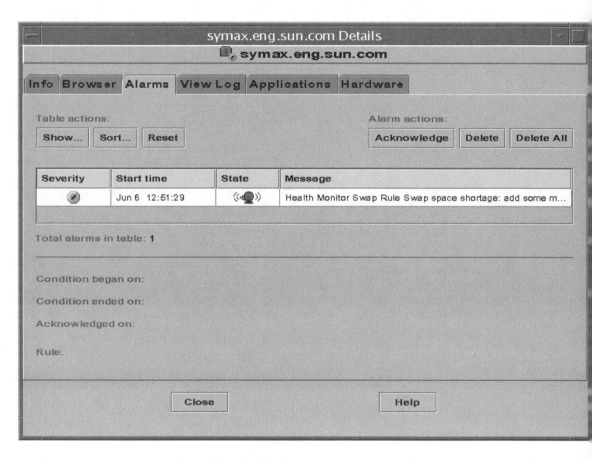

FIGURE 6-6   Alarms Details Window

The next step is to select one or all of the alarms and acknowledge them by clicking the Acknowledge button. It is best to select them all and acknowledge them all at once. It takes some time to perform the acknowledgment, since it involves communicating all the way back to the agent on the server being monitored. Once an alarm is acknowledged, a check mark appears next to it, as shown in FIGURE 6-7.

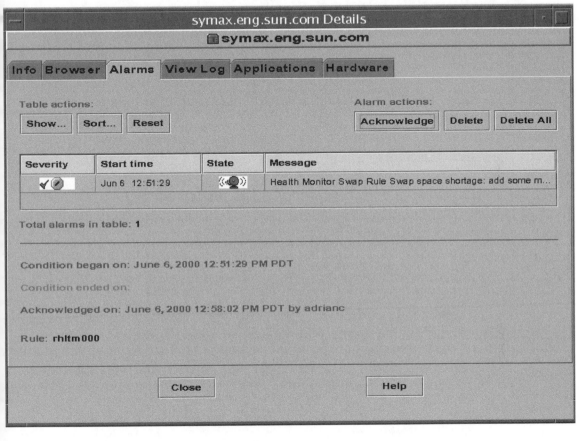

FIGURE 6-7 Acknowledged Alarms

If the Alarms Details window is now closed and you return to the Domain Status Details window, the latter may not have changed. Click the Refresh Now button and the alarm entry will go away. You can now close this window. Look back at the Domain Console and notice that the server no longer has a yellow marker on it and the Domain Status Summary is all zeroes.

The Sun BluePrints book *Resource Management* shows how to separate and monitor multiple workloads with SunMC. Use this capability to track application processes and define alarms that will tell you when something goes wrong—for example, when a process goes away or a workload starts to use too much CPU.

Key Performance Indicator Plots

Operations must have access to displays that show daily data for the main components of key systems. These are a great help with problem diagnosis. A simple approach is to log data to a table, import it into a spreadsheet, and plot the key indicators. It is also possible to automatically generate plots on a Web page by using free tools such as MRTG (Multi Router Traffic Grapher, www.mrtg.org) and Orca (www.orca.net). The disadvantage of these methods is that they do not operate in real time and need to be refreshed manually. Almost all commercial performance tools supply data in real time for display in ways that are suitable for an operations monitoring display.

An example of a useful display is a spreadsheet that reads in data logged to a file using the SE toolkit. This spreadsheet is available for download at http://www.sun.com/blueprints/tools. In this spreadsheet, plots cover the main components of a single system, such as CPU, disk, network, and memory. The following plots are displayed in the next five figures:

- FIGURE 6-8 and FIGURE 6-9 show CPU utilization, the balance of user CPU time to system CPU time, and the load average (number of runnable jobs) relative to the number of CPUs configured and online.

- FIGURE 6-10 shows disk utilization for the busiest disk in the whole system and the average utilization over all the disks in the system. This graph shows how skewed the load is, and highlights the most likely disk bottleneck. Read and write throughput in KB/s shows the data transfer characteristics.

- FIGURE 6-11 displays network throughput in KB/s. This number can be obtained either by monitoring the TCP stack or by monitoring the network interfaces. Most interfaces report byte-level counters these days, but many tools just read packet-level information, which is far less useful, given the wide range of possible packet sizes.

- FIGURE 6-12 displays memory and swap space; they can be plotted together, but need to be interpreted differently. Swap space must always be available so that processes can start and grow, because if a process runs out, the system will have problems. Main memory is managed by reclaiming itself once it reaches a low threshold, so it will tend to hover around that threshold. The page residence time is another useful measure, as explained here.

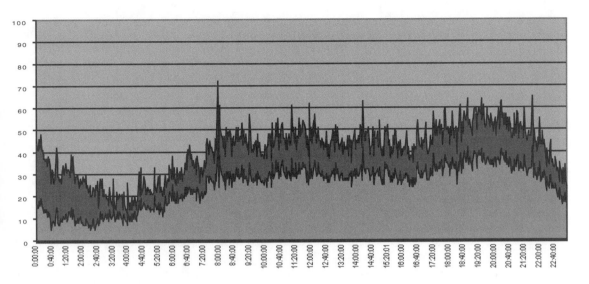

FIGURE 6-8   CPU User and System Time for a Day

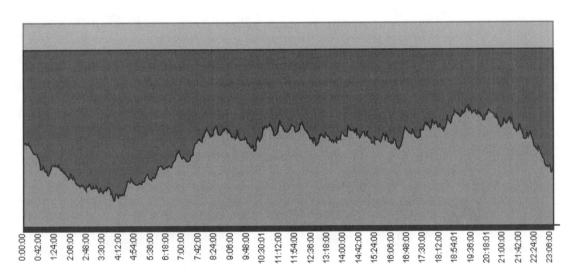

FIGURE 6-9   Five-Minute Load Average and Number of CPUs Online

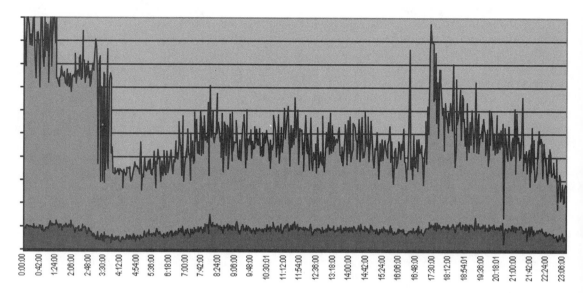

FIGURE 6-10 Disk Utilization – Busiest Disk and Average Over All Disks

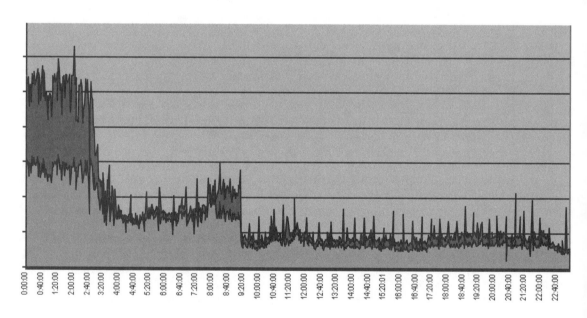

FIGURE 6-11 Disk Throughput Read and Write KB/s

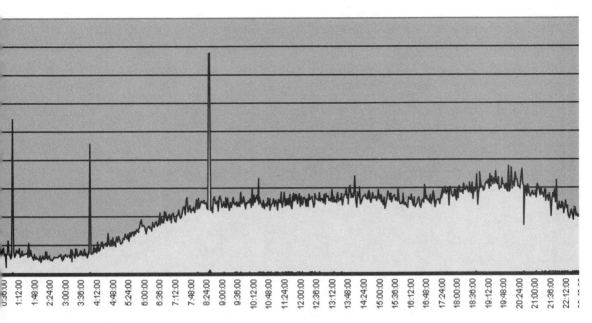

FIGURE 6-12 Network Throughput Over a Day

The network plot shows a few spikes of high throughput because of file transfers taking place on a local fast network, but its overall shape follows the load average fairly closely in this case. The characteristics of these plots show that this system is active all the time, and it has a load shape that is typical of many Internet sites. The system is quiet overnight, gets busy and plateaus during the day, then peaks in the early evening. The CPU and disk plots also show that there is extra system CPU time during the night and a higher disk data rate associated with an online backup taking place. The axis scales have been removed from some of these plots, partly to obscure the source of the example data and because the absolute values are less important than the changes in shape from day to day.

The memory plots below show a regular batch job creating and deleting a large file, and memory and swap space being regularly consumed and freed (see FIGURE 6-13). There are a few times when the page residence time drops to a low level during the backup period. This value is calculated by dividing the page scan rate into a system parameter called the handspread pages. Since the scan rate can be zero, a divide by zero is caught, and the residence time is clamped to 600 seconds (see FIGURE 6-14). Sustained residence times of 30 seconds or less can be a problem with older Solaris OE releases. An optional setting for Solaris 7 OE (which is also included in the kernel patch for Solaris 2.6 and 2.5.1 OEs) turns on priority paging. When enabled, much higher page scan rates can be sustained without problems because the file cache pages are reclaimed before executable code, stack, and heap pages. The rule should be modified to have five seconds as the problem level for residence time when "`priority_paging = 1`" is set in the kernel. Solaris 8 OE uses a completely different algorithm, which allows the file cache to be included in the free memory value, and the absolute value of free memory to be used directly to see how much memory capacity is available for use. In Solaris 8 OE, scanning only occurs when the system is extremely short of memory.

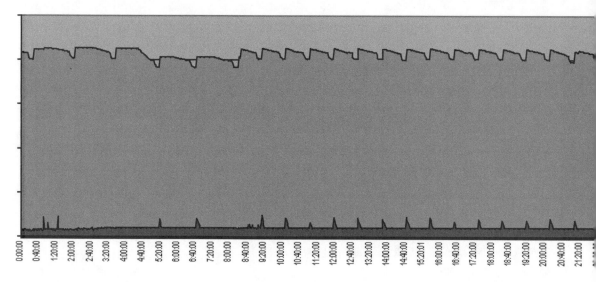

FIGURE 6-13 Memory and Swap Usage

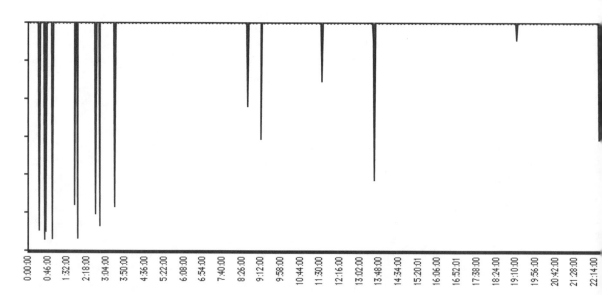

FIGURE 6-14 Memory Demand Viewed as Page Residence Time

Operations Viewpoint Implementations Summary

Operations monitoring concentrates on real-time, alert-based problem diagnosis. It can be implemented with a variety of tools and displays along the lines described above. Its requirements are quite different from those of capacity planners and management reports, although it feeds information to both of them.

Management Viewpoint Implementation

In this section, we describe a weekly report for management. It is constrained to a single sheet of paper and provides "at a glance" status information for future scenarios, as well as an overview of the previous week. The report must be customized to your own situation, so we describe the construction and reasoning behind the report in detail.

For this discussion, managers are assumed to have the following characteristics:

- They assign resources that can affect project schedules.
- They approve capital equipment purchases.
- They have a short attention span for technical issues, but need to be able to summarize any externally visible problems to analysts and investors.
- They like to be informed about what is happening, but it is more important to tell them when they need to take action on and what options they have.
- They are seemingly incapable of turning over a piece of paper or scrolling down a Web page to look through a whole report.
- They are quite likely to glance at a single sheet of colorful paper, especially if it has lots of red on it.

The example report shown in FIGURE 6-15 is customized for use by a large Internet e-commerce site where the primary bottleneck is a large back-end database server. For many consumer-oriented sites, Monday has the highest load of the week, so the report is designed to be delivered each Tuesday. It covers from Monday of the previous week to the Monday before the report and predicts whether there is enough site capacity to survive the load expected for the following Monday. The report is in four sections:

1. A short text summary of issues and noteworthy events

2. A colored dashboard table showing the status of future scenarios

3. A colored table showing the daily status over the last week and a chart showing the level of activity over the last week

4. An excerpt from an external site testing service, such as Keynote, that measures site availability and performance

Weekly Status Report: April 18, 2000

The site ran fairly smoothly the past week. A new record bandwidth of 253.8 Mbit/s was seen on Monday night. User-visible problems caused by nightly backup overrunning into daytime operation on 14, 17, and 18th. Currently, no configuration changes may go into the site without first being approved by the team working on this issue. The schedule for hardware upgrade on 12-May is at risk due to component delivery lead times

Load and Capacity Increase Scenarios and Primary Bottleneck Utilization

Date		17-Apr	12-May	20-May	14-Jun	21-Jul	23-Aug
Load Increase	Event	Current	HW Upgrade 22%	App V2.6 36%	OS Upgrade 15%	DBMS Up 25%	App V3.0 80%
18-Apr	Current	71%	58%	43%	37%	30%	17%
24-Apr	Next Monday	65%	53%	39%	34%	27%	15%
29-May	Five Weeks	92%	75%	55%	48%	39%	21%
16-Jun	Mktg Push	120%	98%	72%	63%	50%	28%
17-Jul	Three Months	110%	90%	66%	58%	46%	26%
23-Oct	Six Months	185%	152%	111%	97%	78%	43%
17-Apr	Next Year	447%	366%	269%	234%	187%	104%

Last Week Status, Problem Severity and Count Overview, and Graph

Problem Status and Counts	Mon 10-Apr	Tuesday 11-Apr	Weds 12-Apr	Thurs 13 -Apr	Friday 14-Apr	Saturday 15-Apr	Sunday 16-Apr	Monday 17-Apr	Tuesday 18-Apr
Problems Total	15	14	14	13	12	15	16	12	10
Resolved / New	6 / 3	3 / 2	3 / 3	4 / 3	5 / 5	1 / 4	2 / 3	7 / 3	5 / 3

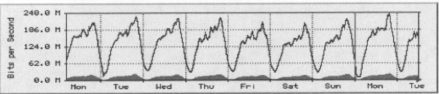

AVAILABILITY (Availibility Rating: * * * * *) and PERFORMANCE (Performance Rating: * * * * *)

Percentage of Successful Page Downloads		Average Download Time	
99.43%	Successful Downloads of Site Specific page	1.12 sec	Download Time for Site Specific Page
96.28%	Successful Downloads of Standardized Page	2.55 sec	Download Time for Standardized Page

FIGURE 6-15 Example Management Status Report

Weekly Summary

Summarize the week's activity into four or five lines of text (see FIGURE 6-16).

Weekly Status Report: April 18, 2000

The site ran fairly smoothly the past week. A new record bandwidth of 253.8 Mbit/s was seen on Monday night. User-visible problems caused by nightly backup overrunning into daytime operation on 14, 17, and 18th. Currently, no configuration changes may go into the site without first being approved by the team working on this issue. The schedule for hardware upgrade on 12-May is at risk due to component delivery leadtimes.

FIGURE 6-16 Management Report: Weekly Summary Section

This summary indicates that user-visible problems over the past week were caused by the nightly online backup taking too long and spilling over into the high-load daytime period, where it adversely affected user response times. It also notes a possible schedule slip for the next site upgrade, so that senior managers can expect to be involved in contingency planning and supplier meetings to firm up the schedule.

Scenario Planning

The entire capacity planning process is described in more detail in Chapter 4, "Scenario Planning." The output from the scenario planning process includes a schedule of upgrade events that increase site capacity and a schedule of expected increases in load. The important messages to convey to management are whether there will be enough capacity to handle the load in the future, and how they should manage resources and schedules to keep the site running.

The weekly report is delivered on Tuesday so that there is time to make and test any changes needed to cope with the expected peak on the following Monday. The entire capacity plan is recalculated once a week, based on updated information about schedules and expected performance improvements. Taking new current data as a baseline, the recalculation also updates the first column with the projected future dates.

The capacity plan is based on a simple primary bottleneck scenario. The utilization is shown as a percentage for each scenario. Scenarios that are at risk due to schedule slips are colored yellow; scenarios that will have enough capacity are colored green and scenarios that are over 90% busy are colored red. The load increases rapidly with time and takes into account seasonality effects and a marketing campaign that is labelled "Mktg Push." The load starts at 71%, and actually decreases slightly to 65% the following week due to a seasonal lull. In five weeks time on 29-May, the load will be 92% with the current site configuration. A hardware upgrade is scheduled for 12-May and the effect of this upgrade is shown in the second column

The upgrade is estimated to give a 22% performance increase, which (if implemented the day of the report [Tues., 18-Apr]) would reduce the 71% utilization to 58%. If the hardware upgrade was implemented the following week, it would reduce 65% to 53%, and in five weeks, it would reduce the 92% utilization to 75%. However, the schedule for this upgrade is at risk, and if it slips from 12-May back to near 29-May, there will not be enough capacity to cope with the load, hence the yellow status indicator. Similarly, an application code for an upgrade to Version 2.6, ("App V2.6") scheduled on 20-May is expected to give a 36% performance boost. This must be scheduled before the "Mktg Push" on 16-Jun, and it is currently on track.

To give a target for the long term, the last row estimates the capacity requirements in a year's time. This helps encourage the formation of large projects that have a long lead time but a significant impact, such as the "App V3.0" improvement of 80% in the last column (see FIGURE 6-17). This project might involve splitting functionality over several systems to reduce the amount of work being routed to the primary bottleneck.

Load and Capacity Increase Scenarios and Primary Bottleneck Utilization

Date		17-Apr	12-May	20-May	14-Jun	21-Jul	23-Aug
Load Increase	Event	Current	HW Upgrade 22%	App V2.6 36%	OS Upgrade 15%	DBMS Up 25%	App V3.0 80%
18-Apr	Current	71%	58%	43%	37%	30%	17%
24-Apr	Next Monday	65%	53%	39%	34%	27%	15%
29-May	Five Weeks	92%	75%	55%	48%	39%	21%
16-Jun	Mktg Push	120%	98%	72%	63%	50%	28%
17-Jul	Three Months	110%	90%	66%	58%	46%	26%
23-Oct	Six Months	185%	152%	111%	97%	78%	43%
17-Apr	Next Year	447%	366%	269%	234%	187%	104%

FIGURE 6-17 Management Report: Scenario Planning Summary

Weekly Problem Summary

This section gives a view of events over the previous week or so (see FIGURE 6-18).
includes both problem counts and a graph of activity from Monday of the previou
week through to about midday the next Tuesday.

Last Week Status, Problem Severity and Count Overview, and Graph

Problem Status and Counts	Mon 10-Apr	Tuesday 11-Apr	Weds 12-Apr	Thurs 13 -Apr	Friday 14-Apr	Saturday 15-Apr	Sunday 16-Apr	Monday 17-Apr	Tuesday 18-Apr
Problems Total	15	14	14	13	12	15	16	12	10
Resolved / New	6 / 3	3 / 2	3 / 3	4 / 3	5 / 5	1 / 4	2 / 3	7 / 3	5 / 3

FIGURE 6-18 Management Report: Weekly Problem Summary

The first row gives the total number of problems that were unresolved at the end ⊂
each day. It also color-codes the overall status of the day according to the severity ⊂
problems that occurred at any time during the day. In this case, three days are
shown yellow because backups overran and affected daytime operation.

The second row shows how many problems were resolved during a day and how
many new problems were registered. If staff are being overwhelmed with so many
problems that the problems are not being analyzed and resolved, then the status
would turn yellow or red in the second row, and the problem count would keep
increasing in the first row. Problems can occur at a relatively constant rate
throughout the week on average, but analysis and resolution tend to take place
during the week when all the staff are available. This means that the total problem
count may tend to accumulate over the weekend and drop back quickly at the star
of the week.

The graph is aligned to the daily problem summary. This particular graph was
obtained from a freely available tool called MRTG, which is monitoring the total
Internet-connected bandwidth of this site. The bandwidth drops to near zero just
after midnight on Sunday; this drop corresponds to a scheduled maintenance
downtime. Looking at the load pattern, we see this is not a good time to take the si*
down. It might be better to schedule downtime at a different time, for example,

Thursday night/Friday morning. For this site, that would correspond to the lightest load on a Friday and would have the least business impact if problems occurred during or after the maintenance period. There is also a good system administration principle of not changing anything during Friday, so that you don't have to work the weekend sorting out any problems!

External Monitoring Summary

Several companies provide external monitoring services for Web sites; the best known is Keynote Corp (www.keynote.com). Keynote uses connections from many parts of the Internet so that they cover a sample of the end-user population. They contact the site being tested at regular intervals, count how many times they get a response, and measure the response time. Two kinds of Web pages on a site can be tested: a standardized page that allows comparisons between Web sites, and a site-specific page that tests the functionality of the actual Web site and any back-end systems that may be involved. Other vendors in this market are Mercury Interactive (www.mercury.com) and Envive Corp (www.envive.com). In addition to measuring availability and performance in normal operation, Mercury and Envive also provide a load testing service that can be used to stress-test sites before they go into production or to apply a stress test during low-load periods.

A full Keynote report covers the performance of many components of the Web site, which is measured from many parts of the Internet. For the management report, a single measurement is sufficient, as shown in FIGURE 6-19.

AVAILABILITY(Availability Rating: * * * * *) and PERFORMANCE(Performance Rating: * * * * *)			
Percentage of Successful Page Downloads		Average Download Time	
99.43%	Successful Downloads of Site Specific page	1.12 sec	Download Time for Site Specific Page
96.28%	Successful Downloads of Standardized Page	2.55 sec	Download Time for Standardized Page

FIGURE 6-19 Management Report: Site Availability and Performance Summary

This report was constructed to illustrate the principles involved in this example. Management reports need to be customized to the exact situation at hand.

Engineering Viewpoint Implementation

Engineering groups include capacity planning, application development, system administration, database administration, and vendor service and presales systems engineers. They are responsible for recommending upgrades, system performance tuning, application tuning, and problem diagnosis. Hence, large amounts of detaile performance data need to be collected and analyzed.

Most performance tools collect a large number of system statistics, but there are some common areas of weakness. Commercial tools try to support several version of UNIX systems in a generic manner and tend to skip anything that is specific to one particular implementation. For a full and detailed picture of what is happenin on a Solaris OE system, additional information generally needs to be collected. The SunMC product provides data on some of the Sun specific capabilities; in particula it has very detailed configuration information. However, it does not include all possible data sources and currently does not include a performance database for long-term historical data storage. Some of the additional data that should be collected is listed below:

- `sar` data

    The standard system utility `sar` is already set up through `cron` to collect dat at regular intervals; it just needs to be enabled. The `sar` data files are collecte in the directory `/var/adm/sa` and should be archived to a long-term storage location because the default collection scripts overwrite data after one month The `sar` data file contains disk information as well as many of the system an virtual memory counters accumulated over all CPUs.

- TCP network statistics

    This measurement should include connection rates, TCP byte-level throughpu and retransmission rates. The raw counters can be obtained from `netstat -` output or through SNMP. The counters must be read and compared frequentl enough to avoid counter values wrapping around.

- Detailed network interface statistics

    The default statistics for each network interface include only packet and erro counters and a collision rate. Since most modern networks are switched, collisions rarely occur. Additionally, interfaces such as the Sun 100 Mb Etherne `hme` and `qfe` and the Gigabit Ethernet `ge` collect many detailed metrics that are not reported by the `netstat` utility. It is important to obtain byte count throughput metrics for capacity planning; but in addition, there are buffer overflow counters that show when packets are being dropped because of an input overrun.

- Volume manager information

  This information should show the throughput for each volume. The Sun Solstice DiskSuite product provides these volumes with the normal `iostat` tool and `kstat` mechanisms, but some tools do not understand or report the metadevice (md) entries correctly. The VxVM requires that the `vxstat` command be run separately for each disk group that is configured on the system.

- Web server access logs

  These logs provide a useful source of performance information. Sometimes the log can be configured to measure connection times so that response time is measured directly. Operation counts for the HTTP protocol and counts of the number of times particular cgi-bin scripts are run can usefully characterize the workload mix for a site.

- Detailed CPU activity metrics

  These metrics are only reported by the per-CPU `mpstat` tool. Particularly, interrupt counts (`intr`), cross-calls (`xcal`), and mutex stalls (`smtx`) should be collected.

The overhead of collecting data from the system utilities such as `sar`, `iostat`, `netstat`, `mpstat`, and `vxstat` is low as long as the collection interval is set to a reasonable level, such as 30 seconds, and data is logged directly to disk files. The best organization on disk is to build a collection script that maintains a daily directory that contains data files for each tool for each hour, for example:

```
/var/adm/data/16-04-2000/10:00_iostat
```

It is easy for this data to add up to many megabytes per day, so make sure there is enough space, and archive at regular intervals.

SE Orcollator Logs

One approach to data collection is to use the SE toolkit to build a custom data collector that includes whatever data you like and stores it in any format that you find convenient. The best starting point is the `orcollator.se` script, which is in use at many Sun based Internet sites. This script was developed from Adrian Cockcroft's original `percollator.se` script by Blair Zajac while he was working at the GeoCities Web site. Blair also developed the Orca Web-based data plotting tool. The disadvantage of using the SE toolkit is that it is unsupported free code. You must devote some engineering resources to maintaining the SE scripts yourself, but since you probably already have shell scripts that collect performance data, some additional scripts may not be a problem.

SAS Data Import and Analysis

SAS (www.sas.com) is a general-purpose statistics package that is widely used to analyze and report computer performance data in the mainframe world. It is particularly useful as a central place to consolidate data from many other tools. Tw main add-on packages customize SAS for use as a capacity planning tool: the SAS I Service Vision (SAS/ITSV) package, which was originally called SAS/CPE; and MXG (www.mxg.com) by Barry Merrill. SAS/ITSV has very good graphical and data analysis capabilities, but it is tricky to write the data import utilities needed t get arbitrary data into the system. If you purchase SAS, it is a good idea to also purchase some SAS consultancy to build data import scripts for all the data source to get them into SAS/ITSV format. MXG primarily focuses on mainframe-oriented data import and analysis; however, discussions have taken place between Adrian Cockcroft and Barry Merrill, and some Sun/Solaris OE data can be imported from orcollator data files to MXG for analysis.

Summary

This chapter concentrated on the requirements for information collection and presentation to three different audiences. Some tools were mentioned in passing; th next chapter presents a more in-depth survey of useful tools for capacity planning

Tools Overview and Evaluations

Sun's own tools are currently focused on system management monitoring and availability. Third-party tools include performance databases and trending and modelling capabilities. Over time, more of these functions are likely to be integrated into Sun's product line.

This chapter describes several useful Sun and third-party tools for capacity planning. It also offers several ways to balance peak load both within and across systems to eliminate underutilization and maximize IT computing resources.

Tools and Products for Performance Management

By combining service definition monitoring and the ongoing task of performance monitoring, an IT department can easily begin identifying utilization trends and resource restrictions within its networks and servers. Analysis of this information may reveal that many systems are either underutilized or seriously strained during peak loads. Fortunately, there are a number of ways to smoothly balance the load both within and across systems to maximize IT computing resources.

Server Consolidation

Server consolidation has become a popular endeavor for IT departments to decrease the datacenter space, simplify management, increase reliability, and decrease costs. By analyzing the resource requirements of multiple applications on distinct servers, you may be able to consolidate those services on fewer machines. By analyzing the services that are currently running in the datacenter, you may be able to identify services that would be prime candidates for consolidation.

Remember to analyze the service requirements carefully and ensure that the new system can handle the load of the combined services during the peak hours. Also, on the lookout for batch jobs and reports to make sure that the system can handle the requests from multiple competing services. If a defined approval process or schedule for starting batch jobs and recording their duration and resource usage is not in place, institute one so that service levels can be managed for batch and online activity.

Domains and Dynamic Reconfiguration

There are occasions when server consolidation is desired, but because of resource application constraints, it may not be desirable to run multiple services on a single instance of Solaris OE. More than one version of Solaris OE will need to be supported as applications transition to support newer releases.

In these cases, a Sun Enterprise 10000 server with domains and DR may be the ideal solution. By creating discrete domains within the Sun Enterprise 10000 server, each with its own version of Solaris OE, you may be able to consolidate many different services into the server. The added benefit of DR also enables you to move a system board containing memory and CPUs from one domain to another. This feature is ideal when one domain needs additional computing power, say, for a large report, and another domain has an idle time period and does not need the extra resources.

Solaris Resource Manager

DR in the Sun Enterprise 10000 server provides discrete "hard" partitioning of domains, whereas SRM software provides a way to distribute CPU and virtual memory to specific applications or users within a single image of Solaris OE. These resource allocations act as a form of "soft" partitioning; that is, they carve up resources in a single instance of Solaris, whether it is on a single server or a Sun Enterprise 10000 server domain.

This tool can be extremely useful when you combine mixed workload applications on a single server. To illustrate how this works, let's look at the following example:

> Assume a server is running a database that serves both interactive users and batch processing of reports. During the day, 300 users are online and the system is at 70% utilization. At night, the department manager runs daily reports and trending reports that consume about 85% of the machine's resources. For reasons unknown, the manager decides to run the reports in the middle of the day. The result is invariably very poor response for the interactive users.

At the end of the year, the manager also needs to run the annual reports. Unfortunately, business was so good this year that the batch job does not finish during the night; so when the users come into work the next morning, the response time is, again, very poor. At this point, there are really only two possibilities for the administrator: 1) suspend the report, or 2) have the users suffer.

The SRM software enables the administrator to establish resource usage policies for the CPU and virtual memory resources, so priorities can be established to prevent these problems. By the interactive users being alloted an 80% share and the batch processes a 10% share of the resources during working hours, the users will have a normal day. When they all go to lunch or the machine has an idle moment, the batch process is allowed to use those idle resources, since the CPU share constrains the system only when it is oversubscribed. When the users come back, the batch job instantly relinquishes the CPU for their use. At night, the administrator can set up a different rule that gives the batch process the lion's share of the resources and constrains the interactive users, thereby giving the batch process priority in case users leave some CPU-intensive jobs of their own running overnight.

Note that even though a database was used in this example, any application can be controlled by the SRM software. This capability is particularly useful when the user population is "out of control" and can be used to constrain CPU-related denial-of-service problems on Web sites. In addition, it can be used to ensure that fee-paying subscribers get better service levels than casual or guest users. When multiple Web sites are hosted on a single server, a common problem is that poorly written cgi-bin scripts and searches from a single Web site can saturate the server and affect the performance of all the other sites. The SRM software can be used to give each site its own equal share, so that no one site can dominate the system.

Solaris Bandwidth Manager

In many ways, the Solaris Bandwidth Manager (SBM) software provides the same capability for network bandwidth that the SRM software provides for CPUs and virtual memory. It allows the administrator to establish controls for the amount of bandwidth that applications, users, and departments are allowed to use. The SBM software provides the framework for quality of service (QoS) guarantees and SLAs for critical networked applications.

One example of using the SBM software to guarantee compliance with a QoS or SLA could be a corporate intranet server that provides both Web and ftp data. For instance, in the middle of the day, a user decides to ftp every file found on the server. The Web users will start experiencing greater latency as the ftp server starts sending files. By establishing rules in the SBM software, the administrator can guarantee enough network bandwidth by throttling the ftp traffic. It is also possible to manage according to the destination of the traffic. A server can be dedicated to give the best service to a certain class of users that have a specified network address. This can be useful in corporate intranets and can also be used to constrain denial-of-service attacks on the network without shutting off access completely. For example, if a hacker uses a large ISP (Internet service provider) to attack your site by flooding it with packets, you could deny all access from that site fairly easily, but this would upset legitimate users. With the SBM software, you can limit the incoming bandwidth from a certain ISP to a data rate that you can handle, and then work to filter out very specific types of packets that are coming from the hacker.

Load Sharing Facility and Codeine

The load sharing facility (LSF) from Platform Computing Corporation is a tool that takes advantage of idle CPU cycles on a network to assist with batch processes. This tool is most useful in environments that have intensive technical batch applications like simulations. LSF may be the right tool to allow IT departments to meet batch requirements in an SLA.

LSF uses a cluster model for implementation. There are three roles to which hosts can be assigned within a cluster, and hosts can have more than one role:

- Master host – Maintains information about all other hosts in the cluster and the batch queues.
- Submission host – Accepts requests from users for a batch process.
- Execution host – Processes the request (or a piece of the request).

LSF enables users to submit batch jobs and gives the administrator the capability to set up rule sets to prioritize the requests.

Codeine is a similar product developed by Gridware. In mid-2000, Sun acquired Gridware and is integrating Codeine into the Sun product line.

Sun Management Center (SunMC)

This product is described in more detail in "Implementing with Sun Management Center" on page 120. Earlier versions of the product were known as Sun Enterprise SyMON software. To obtain more information and to download a version that works on a single system, go to http://www.sun.com/software/sunmanagementcenter. An additional license is required to manage multiple systems, and SunMC can be used to manage hundreds of systems running Solaris 2.5.1, 2.6, 7, and 8 OEs from a single console.

SunMC Hardware Diagnostic Suite 1.0

SunMC Hardware Diagnostic Suite 1.0 is a comprehensive, network-aware diagnostics tool that enhances overall availability by detecting hardware faults before systems are affected and by reducing routine system maintenance through scheduled testing. This module is free of charge to download from http://www.sun.com/software/sunmanagementcenter/hwds/ and is an add-on solution for SunMC.

SunMC Hardware Diagnostic Suite enhances system availability by:

- Finding hardware faults before the system is affected
- Reducing (or eliminating) routine system maintenance time

SunMC Hardware Diagnostic Suite achieves this goal through three key features:

- Online testing to detect hardware faults
- Test scheduling to enable latent fault detection
- Integration with SunMC for unified system management

Conduct Online Testing While Applications Are Running

With online testing, system administrators can quickly diagnose, detect, and isolate failing components, thereby reducing downtime caused by hardware failure.

The SunMC Hardware Diagnostic Suite enables you to run comprehensive, data-safe, and non-resource-intensive hardware diagnostics testing in enterprise environments while applications are still running. The testing does not corrupt data on the system and uses minimal system resources. Types of online testing include:

- Functional diagnostic testing – Covers device functional testing for processors, memory, network interfaces, disk drives, communication ports (serial and parallel), SPARCstorage Array enclosures, CD-ROM drives, and tape drives.
- Quick check testing – Provides a quick test to see if devices are currently connected to the system.
- Test scheduling for routine system validation or for immediate hardware health checks – Schedules tests to run periodically in the background. Prepackaged test configurations are provided for scheduling to provide convenient system coverage. Scheduled routine hardware validation can replace other maintenance that requires system downtime.

SunMC Integration

SunMC modules tie into the SunMC alarm framework so users can execute corrective action scripts or programs that eliminate faults.

Users have remote access to diagnostic tests through the Java™ technology-based SunMC console, which operates on the Solaris OE and Windows platforms. SunMC 3.0 is the current release and it has a different license model. The base functionalit now works across as many systems as you like, but extra functions such as health monitoring are now provided as add-on packages.

Sun Configuration & Service Tracker

Configuration & Service Tracker (CST) is an online tracking utility that continuously tracks configuration changes of the system on which it is running. CST can be obtained for free from http://access1.sun.com/Products/solaris/cst/. The tracked information is presented in a user-friendly format through a browser-enabled Java applet.

CST fills an important hole in the overall strategy of proactive system managemen at a customer site. It provides a macroscopic view of the system configuration changes caused by failures or upgrades and service patterns over extended periods CST performs these beneficial tasks:

- Reviews configuration consistency at shipping installation and at other times
- Detects incompatible upgrades
- Gets field replaceable unit (FRU) information from a remote environment
- Computes and tracks system availability statistics

CST adopts a three-tier paradigm that includes middleware, a presentation client, and an agent that resides on each system being tracked. The data collected by the agent is managed by the middleware server, which enables clients to access it with Web browser. The client is implemented as a Java applet.

The agent automatically detects events that potentially involve configuration changes. Examples of such events are:

- Boot/reboot, system down, panic
- Install/uninstall of software packages/patches
- Dynamic attach/unattach (not available in CST1.0.)
- Environmental changes detected through system interfaces (not available in CST1.0)

The agent also provides a facility for maintaining an electronic log of service events For each event, the CST agent creates a snapshot of the system configuration and determines the changes since the previous snapshot. It then catalogs the event and changes in a change log file. It also maintains the current snapshot configuration o the system in a configuration file. Both these files—the change log file and configuration file—are maintained in a specific format to permit postprocess extraction of information. CST also notifies the user of each event it detects.

In an enterprise environment, a middleware server daemon receives updates from the various CST agents in the enterprise. It stores them in a central repository. This facilitates manipulation and viewing of data, even if the host is temporarily inaccessible. The server supports an API (application programming interface) that enables users to invoke a Java applet on a Web browser so they can view the configuration report and change log for any host on the network. The user interface also permits users to enter service comments to complement each service event. In addition to viewing the configuration or system changes, CST also permits users to print the data or send it by email.

BMC Patrol and Best/1

BMC sold the Patrol application management framework for many years and recently bought BGS and the Best/1 product line.

BMC Best/1

BGS was a well-established company that built only performance tools. It pioneered the use of performance modelling, starting off on mainframes over 20 years ago, and launching a UNIX-based product in 1993. There are two sides to the Best/1 product: a real-time performance monitor that covers the same ground as many other products, and a performance analysis and prediction tool that is the market leader at the high end. Best/1 is rapidly adding functionality to a range of tools for the mainframe, minicomputer (VAX and AS/400), UNIX (most vendors), and PC (NT and OS/2) platforms. BMC's breadth of coverage puts their products into a market category where large corporations standardize on a vendor and install tools right across the enterprise. The downside of this functionality is that the entry-level cost is at the high end of the scale, both financially and in the time and training required to use a modelling tool effectively.

This tool can be used in a production environment to monitor systems, but it also can be used to set up and automate the entire process of generating regular reports that include the modelling of alternative future scenarios.

Best/1 has a function-based GUI that works well, but is not easy to use. The initial configuration of the tool can be daunting. BMC is working to simplify the configuration; in large installations, training and consultancy support alleviate this problem. Best/1 for UNIX exports data into a PC-based Visualizer performance database. This database also pulls in data from all other types of systems for which BMC has tools. For UNIX-oriented users, it is annoying to have to switch between systems to view all the data. Visualizer can automatically generate reports that are viewable from a Web browser.

Visualizer is one of the few tools that can analyze trend data in terms of cyclic fluctuations. It implements multivariate adaptive statistical filtering (MASF) which is a sophisticated and automated approach to the problems discussed in Chapter 4 "Scenario Planning."

In summary, if you have experience in the way capacity planning is done in the mainframe world and want to merge this knowledge with UNIX-based systems and database performance monitoring, this tool does the job. If you are coming from a typical UNIX system administrator background or are looking for low-priced monitoring tools, you may not be able to justify the investment needed to fully utilize this product.

BMC Patrol

Patrol is a distributed *application management* system. Performance management is only part of the problem to be solved; keeping applications up and running and collecting application-specific measurements are also important roles for Patrol. The product has a good underlying architecture that scales well in large, distributed installations with multiple data storage points and management consoles.

Like SunMC or Best/1, BMC monitors by evaluating rules in a local agent on each node. However, Patrol's rules are more complex, and its predefined *knowledge modules* understand how to manage everything from an Oracle financials database to a Netscape Web server.

Patrol has been criticized for imposing a larger load on the system being managed than do other tools. Their original collection strategy was to run a standard system utility, such as vmstat, and parse the output—a strategy that is less efficient than reading the kernel directly. More recently, Patrol and Best/1 have been merged to use the same highly efficient data collector. Patrol data can be viewed with a Web browser, and Patrol integrates closely with many network and system management tools. Patrol does not include trending and prediction tools; however, future releases of Patrol and Best/1 will become more integrated to provide the best of both products.

BMC is at www.bmc.com.

Foglight Software (RAPS)

Foglight Software was initially known as Resolute Software and more recently has become a division of Quest Software. It competes in the application management space with BMC Patrol. RAPS uses very efficient data collectors and has an advanced distributed storage architecture and a good GUI. Rich Pettit, who built the first SE toolkit while he was at Sun, is now the Chief Performance Architect for RAPS. The rule set that RAPS uses is based on a superset of the virtual_adrian.se script, but the product is a full, distributed, multiplatform tool. People sometimes ask if there are any plans for a fully supported version of the SE toolkit that runs on other platforms as well as on Sun machines, and this is as close as you will get.

Foglight Software is at www.foglight.com.

SAS IT Service Vision (CPE)

SAS has a wide range of statistical analysis products. SAS/CPE has been used to process computer performance data for many years in both mainframe and UNIX environments. It has a much more sophisticated performance database than do other products, with a very wide range of analysis, reporting, and modelling functions. It is often used in conjunction with performance monitoring products from other vendors to provide capacity planning, performance prediction, and reporting capability. The MXG Toolset is a notable alternative to the SAS/CPE functions that also runs on the basic SAS platform.

More information can be found at www.sas.com and www.mxg.com.

Hyperformix/SES Workbench and Strategizer

SES Workbench is a well-established performance simulation tool. The company has recently changed its name to Hyperformix and has focused on adding a professional services capability to assist in capacity planning simulation development. The simulation used is very different from the analytical performance modelling done by BGS Predict and TeamQuest Model (which work by solving a set of equations). With a simulator, you create a model of the components in your system, then drive it with input load levels and wait for the simulation to stabilize over time. Running a simulation is far more resource-intensive than analytical modelling in both setup time and CPU time. If you have a well-constructed simulation, you get much more information than is available from an analytical model. SES Workbench runs on UNIX systems and NT.

To make it easier to construct models of computer systems and networks, SES Strategizer is preconfigured with high-level components that match common system types in some detail. You still need a lot of experience to make good use of the tool, but it is a lot quicker to construct a model. SES Strategizer runs only on Windows NT.

SES is at www.ses.com and www.hyperformix.com.

Aurora Software SarCheck

SarCheck is a relatively inexpensive tool that can be very useful to help with diagnosis in an operations environment. It runs on many platforms, but on Solaris OE it reads data from sar and ps, then writes a detailed explanation of what it sees almost like an essay. SarCheck uses rules that are based on those in Adrian Cockcroft's virtual_adrian.se tool. The output is punctuated with cross references to specific pages in Adrian's Sun Performance and Tuning book for further explanation.

Aurora Software Inc. is at http://www.sarcheck.com.

Capacity Planning with TeamQuest Model

To show the capabilities of this class of tools, we have constructed an example using a product from TeamQuest Corporation (www.teamquest.com). This product has been used effectively by Sun Professional Services to provide a capacity planning study over a time scale of a month or so.

The TeamQuest suite of performance tools includes many useful tools for simplifying the performance management process. Performance data is monitored and recorded in real time, with both reporting and alert features. The data can be viewed live, showing system and workload performance measures, while the data is being recorded in the TeamQuest database. The performance data for a previously recorded period can also be viewed in context, with drill-down capabilities for debugging any performance problems.

The TeamQuest Alert tool can provide performance condition alarms to a central management console system, which alerts performance analysts, system administrators, or capacity planners to retrieve the recorded performance data for the critical period or analyze the real-time condition of the systems with the TeamQuest View tool.

The TeamQuest on the Web tool moves performance data from servers being monitored to a central Web server host, where the performance data can be viewed by a standard Web browser with Java technology support.

The TeamQuest Model tool can take recorded performance data, categorized by a set of defined application sets, called workloads, and provide input for load and capacity planning.

Creating the Model

From the recorded baseline and system inventory, we can create a model of system performance, as shown in FIGURE 7-1. The workloads defined during the baselining process can be refined and assigned attributes of batch, interactive, or transactional loads. The transaction rates and response times can be adjusted to represent actual application measurements if they are known, or they can be estimated with relative counts adjusted by the resource consumption of the workloads.

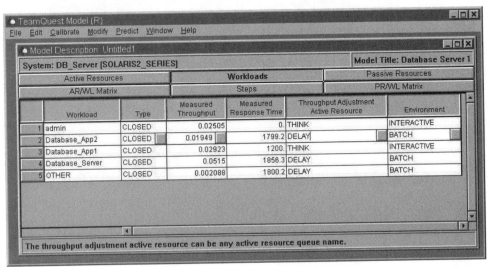

FIGURE 7-1 TeamQuest Model

The system being modelled is a database server, with the database instance and two middleware applications running on the same system. The "admin" workload contains administrative functions, including availability, performance, and application measurement and reporting tools. The "OTHER" workload includes all other work that is being measured, but is not assigned to a specific workload category.

The model can now be adjusted and solved, as shown in FIGURE 7-2, with the variou system active and passive resources assigned to the workloads for each sample period.

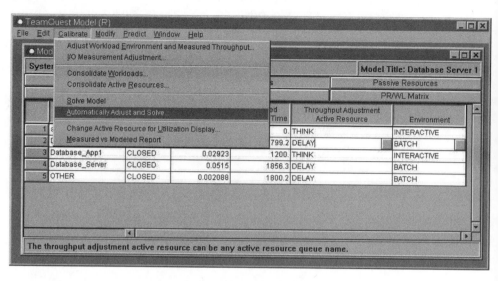

FIGURE 7-2 TeamQuest Model: Adjust and Solve

We will solve the model as accurately as possible and extract the results in a reports window, as shown in FIGURE 7-3. The standard reports produced include several interesting statistics for further analysis. The Principal Results report includes throughput, response time, population, stretch factor, and passive resource (memory or maximum multiprogramming level) statistics.

The Stretch Factor statistic represents the time spent waiting for a resource as compared to the total time spent processing a transaction or unit of work. A higher stretch factor indicates a higher relative quantity of resource wait time. A stretch factor of 1.0 indicates that the workload spent no time waiting for resources and was running at the maximum possible efficiency. Stretch factors greater than 2.0 should be analyzed—they indicate a significant resource shortage with processing time equal to wait time.

The Active Resource report includes resource consumption statistics such as throughput, service time, wait time, average queue length, and number of server instances for each active resource being monitored in the system. Active resources in the example include CPUs, controllers, and disks.

Model Description: Untitled1

System: DB_Server [SOLARIS2_SERIES]   Model Title: Database Server 1

| Active Resources | | Workloads | | | Passive Resources | |
| AR/WL Matrix | | Steps | | | PR/WL Matrix | |

	Workload	Type	Measured Throughput	Measured Response Time	Throughput Adjustment Active Resource		Environment
1	admin	CLOSED	0.02505	0.	THINK		INTERACTIVE
2	Database_App2	CLOSED	0.01949	1799.2	DELAY		BATCH
3	Database_App1	CLOSED	0.02923	1200.	THINK		INTERACTIVE
4	Database_Server	CLOSED	0.0515	1856.3	DELAY		BATCH
5	OTHER	CLOSED	0.002088	1800.2	DELAY		BATCH

Model Reports: Untitled1

System: DB_Server [SOLARIS2_SERIES]   Model Title: Database Server 1

Step Name: Step: 1   Solved at: 23:41:04.00 2000/04/24 by MVAP   Step 1 of 1

| Principal Results | | AR Statistics | | PR Statistics | | Simulation Statistics | |
| WL by AR Statistics | | WL by PR Statistics | | Measured vs Modeled | | Sim Response Time Dist. | |

	Workload	Measured Population	Measured Throughput	Measured Response	Measured CPU%	Modeled Throughput	Modeled Response	Modeled CPU%
1	admin	47.228	0.02505	0.	0.37426	0.02505	1.1334	0.37426
2	Database_App2	35.057	0.01949	1799.2	31.488	0.01942	1787.29	31.381
3	Database_App1	55.332	0.02923	1200.	32.282	0.02915	188.601	32.199
4	Database_Server	95.593	0.0515	1856.3	4.2082	0.05149	1837.91	4.2078
5	OTHER	3.7582	0.002088	1800.2	0.75402	0.002086	1783.26	0.75356

Total measured CPU% = 69.11%; Total modeled CPU% = 68.92%; Model Solved

FIGURE 7-3   TeamQuest Model: Solved With Reports

The Workload by Active Resource Statistics report breaks down the active resources for the system, as reported in the System Active Resource report, and correlates those resources consumed with the workloads configured in the model. Each active resource utilization is reported as a percentage of the system total, simplifying relative process *weight* comparisons. The actual workloads can now be analyzed for independent resource consumption characteristics, as well as for relative resource consumption and possible resource contention between the modelled workloads.

With the calibrated model, we can now add *steps*, defining the projected workload change (see FIGURE 7-4). In this example, the workloads have all been assigned a 5% per month compounded growth factor, which is applied to transaction rates and active resource visits. Active resource visits are counts of the number of discrete accesses to a given resource such as a disk, CPU, controller, or other measured queue.

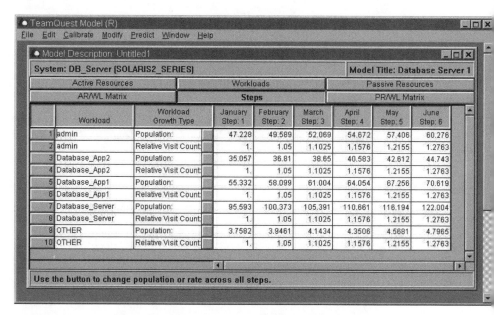

FIGURE 7-4   TeamQuest Model: Steps of Compound Growth Model

The calibrated model, including the new workload growth calculations, can now be exported to create graphs and tables of performance data in Microsoft Excel. The performance data and resource consumptions are then graphed for the system as a whole, and each workload is defined.

The first graph that we will examine is the Stretch Factor by Workload graph (see FIGURE 7-5). This graph shows the projected increase in workload wait time as a portion of total transaction time. The graph shows a column representing each workload for each step (each month has compound 5% growth in this example). The modelled '"Database_App" workloads exhibit a stretch factor of well over 2.0 in the fifth step, sometime during April. The stretch factor increases from just over 2.0 to well over 4.0 in the final step, representing the projected workload for June.

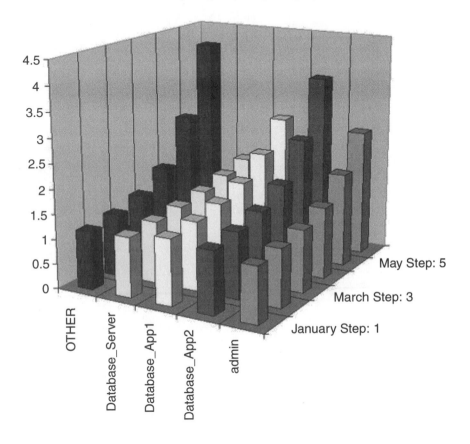

FIGURE 7-5   TeamQuest Model: Workload Stretch Factor Graph

The "Database_App2" workload appears to have a response time increase, which indicates a resource contention problem. This is to be expected, with the increase in relative queue wait time to resource service time represented by the stretch factor.

We can also look at the throughput data and graph for the "Database_App2" workload. From the graph in FIGURE 7-6 and the table data provided from the accompanying spreadsheet, notice that the throughput of the measured workloads increases through the steps. In addition, notice that the "Database_App2" workload has not increased throughput as fast as the proposed workload steps have increased "visit count," or transaction volumes.

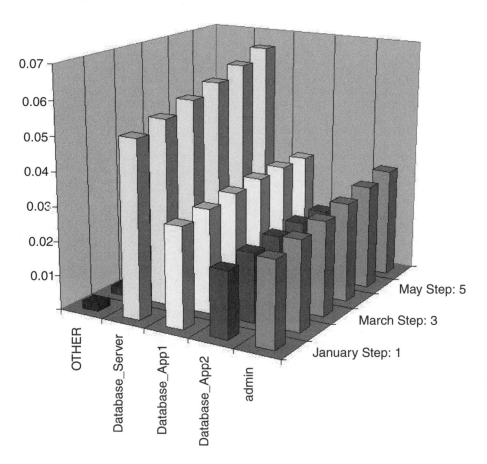

FIGURE 7-6 TeamQuest Model: Workload Throughput Graph

We can further analyze this workload's behavior by using the Components of Response Time graph for the "Database_App2" workload. The graph in FIGURE 7-7 illustrates the time consumed by a transaction, or unit of work within the workload, with time spent in the workload. This is broken down by active resource service time and active resource queue delay. The time between activity in a given workload (while the service is sitting idle), called DELAY time, is removed from these graphs, so we can better analyze the actual resource consumption and resource request delays.

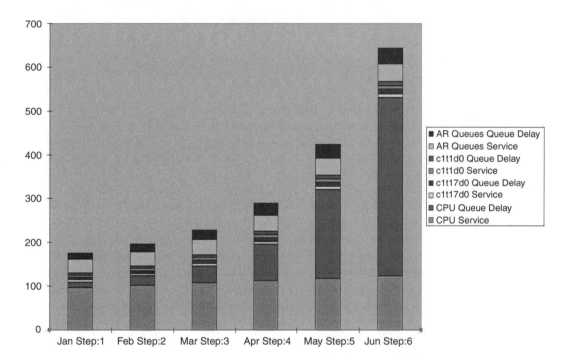

FIGURE 7-7   TeamQuest Model: Components of Response Time for Database_App2

By examining this breakdown of the time spent per transaction in the workload, we can see that the CPU Queue Delay is increasing at an alarming rate and that it accounts for more than half of the per-transaction time by Step 6. This indicates that the system is on the verge of a serious performance degradation if the growth of the workload matches the modelled steps.

In the Active Resource Utilization graph, shown in FIGURE 7-8, we see the busiest system active resources, with the CPU utilization shown to be climbing rather high These values are projected for CPUs in the growth period being modelled, as well a the other busiest system active resources, in this case, disk resources.

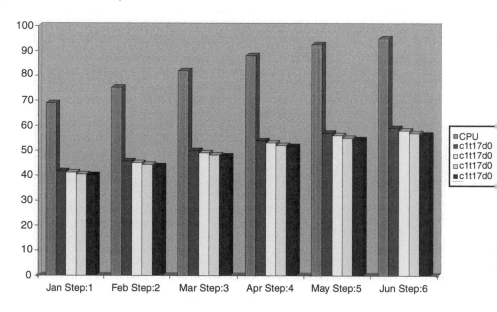

FIGURE 7-8 TeamQuest Model: System Active Resource Utilization Graph

The CPU resource utilization is projected over 95% average utilization by the time the model reaches the sixth step (only five months away). Step 1 shows that we are currently running at approximately 70% utilization, with the active resource utilization for the measured workloads showing very little resource queue delay time (indicating contention for active resources). At Step 2, the workloads are beginning to show some contention and CPU queue delay times, with CPU utilization just passing 75%. This trend would indicate that we should target 70% for the KPI maximum CPU utilization threshold.

To solve this performance trend, we have several choices: we can upgrade the server with more CPUs, faster CPUs, or we could move some of the work from this machine to another server. This modelled system was a Sun Enterprise 10000 server with six 250 MHz UltraSPARC CPUs with 4 MB of E-cache. The chosen solution in this case is to perform a one-to-one upgrade of the CPUs in the system to 400 MHz UltraSPARC CPUs with 8 MB of E-cache using the "Change CPU Name" function of TeamQuest Model, shown in FIGURE 7-9. With this solution, we can return to the TeamQuest Model window, create alternatives based on the current model, called "what if" frames, and modify the system resources to predict the projected performance of the growing workload into the new system configuration.

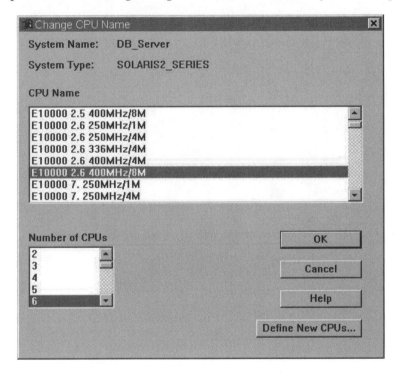

FIGURE 7-9   TeamQuest Model: Change CPU Definition

After recalculating the steps by using the new hardware configuration, we can use the MVAP (Mean Value Approximation Package) Solver to predict the system resource utilization, response times, and queue delays in the new system model by running the same workload steps. Examining the Stretch Factor graph (see FIGURE 7-10) for the new system configuration shows the relative queue delay time for active resources in the new system model.

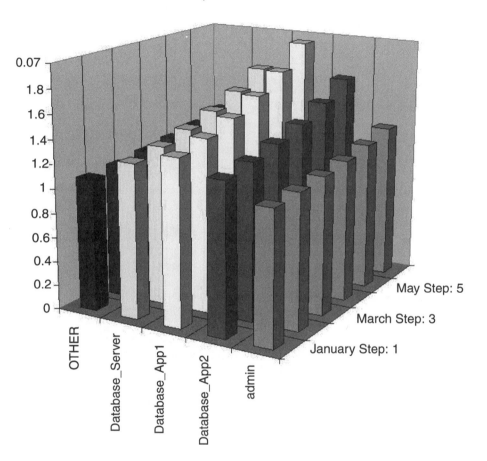

FIGURE 7-10 TeamQuest Model: Upgraded System Stretch Factor Graph

The Stretch Factor graph now shows stretch factors under 2.0 in all steps, for all workloads modelled. In addition, the "Database_App2" workload displays an incremental increase in delay time per unit of work being done. We can delve deeper into the characteristics of the "Database_App2" workload on the new server system model by examining the Resource Component Response Time graph.

The graph in FIGURE 7-11 shows that the CPU wait queue time has been significantly reduced for the "Database_App2" workload as a result of the upgrade; it also shows that the total response time for a unit of work has been greatly reduced in the latter steps of the growth model.

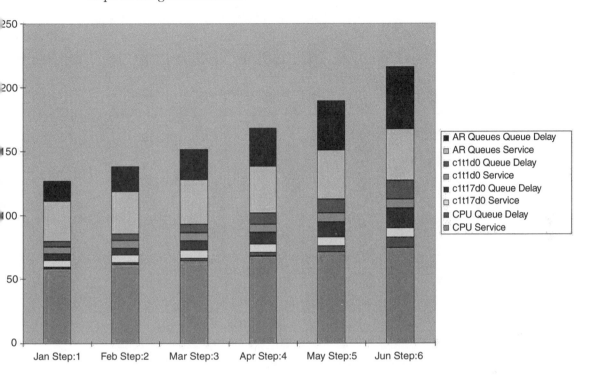

FIGURE 7-11 TeamQuest Model: Upgraded Components of Response Time Graph

We can also examine the total system CPU utilization by looking at the resulting spreadsheet table data or by viewing the Active Resource Utilization graph (see FIGURE 7-12). The CPU and disk active resources are graphed over the current, measured workload, as well as over the five steps of compound growth in the new server platform model.

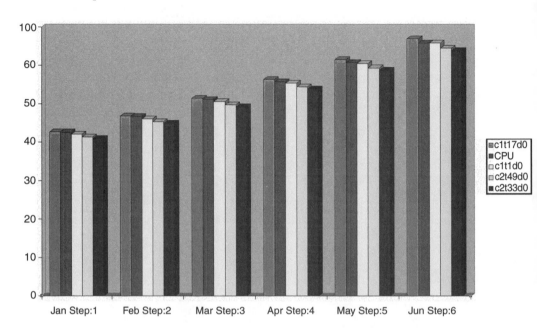

FIGURE 7-12 TeamQuest Model: Upgraded System Active Resource Utilization

The modelled performance in the new server platform shows that CPU utilization is approaching 70% at the end of Step 5, five months into our compound growth model. By projecting this growth and using the previous model with degrading performance in the measured workloads appearing at the 70% CPU utilization threshold, we can plan on another upgrade to the system in approximately five months. We could project the model out even further with additional compound growth steps and use other hardware upgrade scenarios. To maximize the accuracy of the model and account for possible software changes in the workloads, we will continue to monitor and report on the performance of the system. In addition, we will begin a new model at some time in the future, before degradation sets in.

The Active Resource Utilization graph shows that disks are becoming rather busy throughout the model and that disk resource queue delays are starting to appear in the "Database_Server," "Database_App1," and "Database_App2" workloads. We could now return to the model and upgrade the disk subsystems to provide more resource capabilities or move workload resources to balance the disk resources being used.

Summary

This chapter presented a detailed survey of useful tools for capacity planning and discussed the benefits of using both Sun and third-party tools. In addition, this chapter offered several ways to balance peak load both within and across systems to eliminate system strain and underutilization.

Appendix A consists of several tables containing SCPM measurements that indicate the processing potential of system configurations using Solaris OE versions 2.5, 2.5.1, 2.6, 7, and 8.

Sun Constant Performance Metrics

Comparative System Capacity Estimations

The Sun constant performance metric (SCPM) is designed for capacity planning purposes. It indicates the processing potential of a combination of hardware and operating system. The specific intent of the metric is to enable the comparison of dissimilar systems to provide an IT department with an indication of how to plan capacity in a consistent and methodical fashion. In addition to comparing systems, the metric provides a convenient way of expressing the amount of *work* being done by a system.

The metric that SCPM is scaled in is called a quanta (Q). The SCPM is adjusted according to measured performance values obtained with predictable benchmarks.

The trends in SCPM values across the operating system should be examined before upgrades are made. Examining these trends provides guidance for predicting the impact an upgrade may have on system performance. The following measurement tables provide a complete list of comparative system capacity estimations for Solaris versions 2.5, 2.5.1, 2.6, 7, and 8. In the tables, NCPU stands for the number of CPUs.

Solaris 2.5 and 2.5.1 Operating Environment

Enterprise Servers

ESTIMATION TABLE A-1 Enterprise 3000 – Enterprise 6500

NCPU	400/ 8MB	400/ 4MB	336/ 4MB	250/ 4MB	250/ 1MB	167/ 1MB	167/ 512K
1	4210	3900	3300	2750	2290	1740	1650
2	8280	7680	6510	5430	4450	3400	3190
3	12200	11300	9620	8030	6490	4980	4630
4	16000	14900	12600	10500	8400	6470	5970
5	19600	18300	15500	13000	10100	7900	7220
6	23100	21600	18400	15300	11800	9250	8380
7	26500	24900	21100	17700	13400	10500	9460
8	29800	28000	23800	19900	14900	11700	10400
9	33000	31100	26400	22100	16300	12900	11400
10	36100	34000	28900	24200	17700	14000	12200
11	39000	36900	31300	26300	18900	15000	13100
12	41900	39600	33700	28300	20100	16000	13800
13	44600	42300	35900	30200	21200	16900	14500
14	47300	44900	38200	32100	22200	17800	15200
15	49800	47400	40300	33900	23200	18700	15800
16	52300	49900	42400	35700	24100	19500	16400
17	54700	52200	44400	37400	25000	20300	16900
18	57000	54500	46400	39100	25800	21000	17400
19	59200	56700	48300	40700	26500	21700	17900
20	61300	58900	50100	42300	27200	22400	18300
21	63400	61000	51900	43800	27900	23000	18700
22	65400	63000	53700	45300	28500	23600	19100
23	67300	65000	55300	46800	29100	24100	19500
24	69200	66900	57000	48200	29700	24700	19800

ESTIMATION TABLE A-1 Enterprise 3000 – Enterprise 6500 *(Continued)*

NCPU	400/ 8MB	400/ 4MB	336/ 4MB	250/ 4MB	250/ 1MB	167/ 1MB	167/ 512K
25	71000	68700	58500	49500	30200	25200	20100
26	72700	70500	60100	50800	30700	25700	20400
27	74400	72200	61600	52100	31200	26100	20600
28	76000	73900	63000	53400	31600	26600	20900
29	77500	75500	64400	54600	32000	27000	21100
30	79000	77100	65800	55800	32400	27400	21300

ESTIMATION TABLE A-2 Enterprise 10000 (Starfire)

NCPU	400/8MB	400/4MB	336/4MB	250/4MB	250/1MB
1	3920	3630	2970	2360	2120
2	7780	7190	5900	4680	4180
3	11500	10600	8770	6960	6180
4	15300	14100	11500	9200	8120
5	18900	17400	14300	11400	10000
6	22600	20700	17000	13500	11800
7	26100	24000	19700	15700	13600
8	29600	27200	22300	17700	15300
9	33100	30300	24900	19800	16900
10	36500	33400	27400	21800	18600
11	39800	36400	29900	23800	20100
12	43100	39300	32300	25800	21600
13	46300	42200	34700	27700	23100
14	49500	45000	37000	29600	24500
15	52600	47800	39300	31400	25900
16	55700	50600	41500	33300	27300
17	58800	53200	43800	35100	28600
18	61700	55900	45900	36800	29900
19	64700	58500	48100	38500	31100
20	67600	61000	50100	40300	32300
21	70400	63500	52200	41900	33400
22	73200	65900	54200	43600	34600
23	76000	68300	56200	45200	35600

NCPU	400/8MB	400/4MB	336/4MB	250/4MB	250/1MB
24	78700	70600	58100	46800	36700
25	81300	73000	60000	48300	37700
26	83900	75200	61900	49900	38700
27	86500	77400	63700	51400	39700
28	89100	79600	65500	52900	40600
29	91600	81700	67300	54300	41500
30	94000	83800	69000	55800	42400
31	96400	85900	70700	57200	43200
32	98800	87900	72400	58600	44100
33	101000	89900	74000	59900	44900
34	103000	91800	75600	61300	45700
35	105000	93700	77200	62600	46400
36	108000	95600	78800	63900	47100
37	110000	97400	80300	65200	47800
38	112000	99200	81800	66400	48500
39	114000	101000	83300	67600	49200
40	116000	102000	84700	68900	49900
41	118000	104000	86100	70000	50500
42	120000	106000	87500	71200	51100
43	122000	107000	88800	72400	51700
44	124000	109000	90200	73500	52300
45	126000	110000	91500	74600	52800
46	128000	112000	92800	75700	53400
47	130000	114000	94000	76800	53900
48	132000	115000	95300	77800	54400
49	133000	116000	96500	78900	54900
50	135000	118000	97700	79900	55400
51	137000	119000	98900	80900	55800
52	139000	121000	100000	81900	56300
53	140000	122000	101000	82800	56700
54	142000	123000	102000	83800	57100
55	144000	125000	103000	84700	57500
56	145000	126000	104000	85600	57900
57	147000	127000	105000	86500	58300

NCPU	400/8MB	400/4MB	336/4MB	250/4MB	250/1MB
58	148000	128000	106000	87400	58700
59	150000	130000	107000	88300	59100
60	152000	131000	108000	89200	59400
61	153000	132000	109000	90000	59800
62	155000	133000	110000	90800	60100
63	156000	134000	111000	91600	60400
64	157000	135000	112000	92400	60700

Workgroup Servers

ESTIMATION TABLE A-3 Enterprise 250 / Enterprise 450

NCPU	400/2MB	300/2MB	250/2MB
1	3250	2670	2130
2	6420	5260	4110
4	12200	10000	8000

Desktop Servers

ESTIMATION TABLE A-4 Ultra™-2 / Ultra-60 / Ultra-30

NCPU	360/2MB	300/2MB	200/2MB
1	3150	2670	2160
2	5850	4950	4010

ESTIMATION TABLE A-5 Ultra-5 / Ultra-10

NCPU	440/2MB	360/512K	300/512K	266/512K
1	2800	2070	1750	1570

ESTIMATION TABLE A-6 Ultra-1

NCPU	167/512K	143/512K
1	1220	1040

Older Sun Server Systems

ESTIMATION TABLE A-7 SPARCserver™ 1000E / SPARCserver 1000

NCPU	85/1MB	60/1MB	50/1MB	40/1MB
1	648	562	398	349
2	1260	1090	747	653
3	1840	1600	1050	918
4	2380	2080	1320	1140
5	2900	2540	1560	1340
6	3390	2970	1770	1520
7	3850	3380	1950	1670
8	4290	3780	2120	1800

ESTIMATION TABLE A-8 SPARCcenter™ 2000E / SPARCcenter 2000

NCPU	85/2MB	60/2MB	60/1MB	50/2MB	50/1MB	40/1MB
1	755	694	639	588	407	358
2	1480	1370	1260	1160	794	701
3	2190	2040	1870	1730	1160	1020
4	2880	2690	2470	2290	1500	1330
5	3550	3330	3060	2850	1830	1630
6	4200	3960	3640	3390	2150	1920
7	4830	4570	4210	3930	2450	2190
8	5440	5180	4760	4460	2730	2450
9	6030	5770	5300	4980	3000	2700
10	6600	6350	5840	5490	3250	2930
11	7160	6910	6360	6000	3490	3160
12	7700	7470	6870	6490	3720	3380
13	8220	8010	7370	6980	3940	3580
14	8730	8550	7860	7470	4150	3780
15	9220	9070	8340	7940	4340	3970
16	9700	9580	8820	8410	4530	4150
17	10100	10000	9280	8870	4710	4320
18	10600	10500	9730	9330	4880	4480
19	11000	11000	10100	9770	5030	4640
20	11400	11500	10600	10200	5190	4790

ESTIMATION TABLE A-9 SPARCstation™ 20

NCPU	75/1MB	60/1MB	50/1MB	50 no E$
1	576	478	363	262
2	1110	927	705	508
4			1330	

ESTIMATION TABLE A-10 SPARCstation 10 / SPARCserver 600MP

NCPU	50/1MB	40/1MB	40 no E$	40/64K
1	305	256	184	137
2	593	498	358	265
4	1120			360

ESTIMATION TABLE A-11 SPARCstation 2 / SPARCstation IPX

NCPU	40/64K
1	157

Solaris 2.6 Operating Environment

Enterprise Servers

ESTIMATION TABLE A-12 Enterprise 3000 – Enterprise 6500

NCPU	400/ 8MB	400/ 4MB	336/ 4MB	250/ 4MB	250/ 1MB	167/ 1MB	167/ 512K
1	4210	3900	3300	2750	2290	1740	1650
2	8350	7720	6550	5460	4490	3410	3200
3	12400	11400	9740	8130	6580	5010	4670
4	16400	15100	12800	10700	8580	6540	6040
5	20300	18700	15900	13300	10400	8010	7330
6	24100	22200	18900	15800	12300	9410	8550
7	27900	25600	21900	18300	14000	10700	9690
8	31600	29000	24800	20800	15700	12000	10700
9	35300	32300	27600	23200	17300	13200	11700
10	38900	35500	30400	25500	18800	14400	12700
11	42400	38700	33200	27900	20200	15500	13600
12	45800	41700	35900	30100	21600	16600	14400
13	49200	44800	38500	32400	22900	17600	15200
14	52500	47700	41100	34600	24200	18600	15900
15	55800	50600	43600	36800	25400	19600	16600
16	59000	53500	46100	38900	26600	20500	17300
17	62200	56300	48600	41000	27700	21300	17900
18	65300	59000	51000	43100	28700	22100	18500
19	68300	61600	53400	45100	29700	22900	19000
20	71300	64300	55700	47100	30700	23700	19500
21	74200	66800	58000	49100	31600	24400	20000
22	77100	69300	60200	51000	32500	25100	20500
23	79900	71800	62400	52900	33300	25800	20900
24	82700	74100	64500	54800	34100	26400	21300
25	85400	76500	66700	56600	34900	27000	21700

ESTIMATION TABLE A-12 Enterprise 3000 – Enterprise 6500 *(Continued)*

NCPU	400/ 8MB	400/ 4MB	336/ 4MB	250/ 4MB	250/ 1MB	167/ 1MB	167/ 512K
26	88100	78800	68700	58400	35600	27600	22000
27	90700	81000	70800	60200	36300	28200	22300
28	93300	83200	72800	61900	36900	28700	22600
29	95900	85400	74700	63700	37600	29200	22900
30	98400	87500	76700	65300	38200	29700	23200

ESTIMATION TABLE A-13 Enterprise 10000 (Starfire)

NCPU	400/8MB	400/4MB	336/4MB	250/4MB	250/1MB
1	3920	3630	2970	2360	2120
2	7800	7210	5920	4690	4200
3	11600	10700	8830	7000	6230
4	15400	14200	11700	9290	8210
5	19100	17600	14500	11500	10100
6	22800	21100	17300	13800	12000
7	26400	24400	20100	16000	13800
8	30100	27700	22800	18200	15600
9	33600	31000	25500	20400	17400
10	37100	34200	28200	22500	19100
11	40600	37400	30800	24700	20800
12	44000	40600	33400	26800	22500
13	47400	43700	36000	28900	24100
14	50800	46700	38600	30900	25600
15	54100	49800	41100	33000	27200
16	57400	52700	43600	35000	28700
17	60600	55700	46000	37000	30100
18	63800	58600	48400	39000	31600
19	67000	61500	50800	41000	33000
20	70100	64300	53200	42900	34300
21	73200	67100	55600	44900	35700
22	76200	69900	57900	46800	37000
23	79200	72600	60100	48700	38300
24	82200	75300	62400	50500	39500

ESTIMATION TABLE A-13 Enterprise 10000 (Starfire) *(Continued)*

NCPU	400/8MB	400/4MB	336/4MB	250/4MB	250/1MB
25	85100	77900	64600	52400	40700
26	88000	80500	66800	54200	41900
27	90900	83100	69000	56000	43100
28	93700	85700	71200	57800	44200
29	96500	88200	73300	59600	45300
30	99300	90700	75400	61400	46400
31	102000	93100	77500	63100	47400
32	104000	95600	79500	64900	48500
33	107000	97900	81500	66600	49500
34	110000	100000	83500	68300	50500
35	112000	102000	85500	69900	51400
36	115000	104000	87500	71600	52400
37	117000	107000	89400	73200	53300
38	120000	109000	91300	74900	54200
39	122000	111000	93200	76500	55100
40	125000	113000	95000	78100	55900
41	127000	116000	96900	79700	56800
42	130000	118000	98700	81200	57600
43	132000	120000	100000	82800	58400
44	134000	122000	102000	84300	59200
45	137000	124000	104000	85800	59900
46	139000	126000	105000	87300	60700
47	141000	128000	107000	88800	61400
48	143000	130000	109000	90300	62100
49	145000	132000	110000	91700	62800
50	148000	134000	112000	93200	63500
51	150000	136000	114000	94600	64200
52	152000	137000	115000	96000	64800
53	154000	139000	117000	97400	65400
54	156000	141000	118000	98800	66100
55	158000	143000	120000	100000	66700
56	160000	145000	122000	101000	67300
57	162000	146000	123000	102000	67800
58	164000	148000	125000	104000	68400

ESTIMATION TABLE A-13 Enterprise 10000 (Starfire) *(Continued)*

NCPU	400/8MB	400/4MB	336/4MB	250/4MB	250/1MB
59	166000	150000	126000	105000	69000
60	168000	152000	127000	106000	69500
61	170000	153000	129000	108000	70000
62	172000	155000	130000	109000	70500
63	174000	156000	132000	110000	71000
64	175000	158000	133000	111000	71500

Workgroup Servers

ESTIMATION TABLE A-14 Enterprise 250 / Enterprise 450

NCPU	400/2MB	300/2MB	250/2MB
1	3920	3210	2570
2	7730	6340	4960
4	14800	12100	9650

Desktop Servers

ESTIMATION TABLE A-15 Ultra-2 / Ultra-60 / Ultra-30

NCPU	360/2MB	300/2MB	200/2MB
1	3790	3210	2600
2	7040	5970	4830

ESTIMATION TABLE A-16 Ultra-5 / Ultra-10

NCPU	440/2MB	360/512K	300/512K	266/512K
1	3380	2490	2110	1900

ESTIMATION TABLE A-17 Ultra-1

NCPU	167/512K	143/512K
1	1470	1250

ESTIMATION TABLE A-18 SPARCserver 1000E / SPARCserver 1000

NCPU	85/1MB	60/1MB	50/1MB	40/1MB
1	649	610	432	380
2	1260	1190	812	710
3	1840	1740	1140	997
4	2390	2260	1440	1240
5	2900	2760	1700	1460
6	3390	3230	1920	1650
7	3860	3680	2120	1810
8	4290	4100	2300	1960

ESTIMATION TABLE A-19 SPARCcenter 2000E / SPARCcenter 2000

NCPU	85/2MB	60/2MB	60/1MB	50/2MB	50/1MB	40/1MB
1	820	755	694	639	443	389
2	1630	1500	1380	1270	880	775
3	2430	2230	2060	1890	1310	1150
4	3220	2960	2730	2510	1740	1530
5	4010	3690	3390	3120	2160	1900
6	4780	4400	4050	3720	2580	2270
7	5550	5110	4700	4320	2990	2630
8	6310	5800	5340	4910	3400	2990
9	7060	6500	5980	5500	3810	3350
10	7800	7180	6600	6080	4210	3700
11	8540	7850	7230	6650	4610	4050
12	9260	8520	7840	7210	5000	4400
13	9980	9180	8450	7770	5380	4740
14	10600	9840	9050	8330	5770	5080
15	11300	10400	9640	8870	6150	5410
16	12000	11100	10200	9410	6520	5740
17	12700	11700	10800	9950	6890	6070
18	13400	12300	11300	10400	7260	6390
19	14100	13000	11900	11000	7620	6710
20	14700	13600	12500	11500	7980	7020

ESTIMATION TABLE A-20 SPARCstation 20

NCPU	75/1MB	60/1MB	50/1MB	50 no E$
1	626	519	395	285
2	1210	1000	767	552
4			1450	

ESTIMATION TABLE A-21 SPARCstation 10

NCPU	50/1MB	40/1MB	40 no E$
1	331	278	200
2	644	541	390
4	1210		

ESTIMATION TABLE A-22 SPARCstation 2, SPARCstation IPX

NCPU	40/64K
1	156

Solaris 7 and 8 Operating Environment

Enterprise Servers

ESTIMATION TABLE A-23 Enterprise 3000 – Enterprise 6500

NCPU	400/ 8MB	400/ 4MB	336/ 4MB	250/ 4MB	250/ 1MB	167/ 1MB	167/ 512K
1	4210	3900	3300	2710	2360	1880	1670
2	8360	7730	6550	5380	4620	3710	3260
3	12400	11400	9740	8000	6790	5460	4790
4	16400	15100	12800	10500	8870	7160	6240
5	20400	18700	15900	13100	10800	8800	7630
6	24300	22200	18900	15600	12700	10300	8960
7	28200	25700	21900	18000	14600	11900	10200
8	32000	29100	24800	20400	16300	13300	11400
9	35700	32400	27700	22800	18000	14700	12600
10	39400	35700	30500	25100	19600	16100	13700
11	43000	38800	33200	27400	21200	17400	14700
12	46600	42000	35900	29600	22700	18700	15700
13	50100	45000	38600	31800	24100	19900	16700
14	53600	48000	41200	34000	25500	21100	17600
15	57000	51000	43800	36100	26800	22300	18500
16	60300	53900	46300	38200	28100	23400	19300
17	63600	56700	48800	40300	29300	24500	20100
18	66900	59500	51200	42300	30400	25500	20900
19	70100	62200	53600	44300	31500	26500	21600
20	73300	64800	55900	46300	32600	27400	22300
21	76400	67400	58200	48200	33600	28400	23000
22	79500	70000	60500	50100	34600	29300	23600
23	82500	72500	62700	52000	35500	30100	24200
24	85500	74900	64900	53800	36400	31000	24800
25	88400	77400	67000	55600	37300	31800	25300

ESTIMATION TABLE A-23 Enterprise 3000 – Enterprise 6500 *(Continued)*

NCPU	400/ 8MB	400/ 4MB	336/ 4MB	250/ 4MB	250/ 1MB	167/ 1MB	167/ 512K
26	91300	79700	69100	57400	38100	32500	25900
27	94100	82000	71200	59100	38900	33300	26400
28	96900	84300	73200	60800	39700	34000	26900
29	99700	86500	75200	62500	40400	34700	27300
30	102000	88700	77200	64100	41100	35400	27800

ESTIMATION TABLE A-24 Enterprise 10000 (Starfire)

NCPU	400/8MB	400/4MB	336/4MB	250/4MB	250/1MB
1	3920	3630	2970	2360	2120
2	7800	7220	5920	4700	4200
3	11600	10700	8840	7020	6250
4	15400	14200	11700	9330	8250
5	19200	17700	14600	11600	10200
6	22900	21100	17400	13800	12100
7	26600	24500	20200	16100	14000
8	30300	27800	23000	18300	15800
9	33900	31100	25700	20600	17600
10	37500	34400	28400	22800	19400
11	41000	37600	31100	25000	21100
12	44500	40800	33800	27100	22800
13	48000	43900	36400	29300	24500
14	51400	47000	39100	31400	26100
15	54900	50100	41600	33600	27700
16	58200	53100	44200	35700	29300
17	61600	56100	46700	37800	30800
18	64900	59100	49300	39800	32400
19	68200	62000	51700	41900	33800
20	71400	64900	54200	43900	35300
21	74600	67700	56600	46000	36700
22	77800	70600	59100	48000	38100
23	80900	73300	61400	50000	39500
24	84000	76100	63800	52000	40800

NCPU	400/8MB	400/4MB	336/4MB	250/4MB	250/1MB
25	87100	78800	66100	53900	42100
26	90200	81500	68500	55900	43400
27	93200	84200	70800	57800	44600
28	96200	86800	73000	59800	45900
29	99100	89400	75300	61700	47100
30	102000	91900	77500	63600	48300
31	105000	94500	79700	65400	49400
32	107000	97000	81900	67300	50600
33	110000	99400	84000	69200	51700
34	113000	101000	86200	71000	52800
35	116000	104000	88300	72800	53800
36	119000	106000	90400	74700	54900
37	121000	109000	92500	76500	55900
38	124000	111000	94500	78200	56900
39	127000	113000	96600	80000	57900
40	129000	115000	98600	81800	58900
41	132000	118000	100000	83500	59800
42	135000	120000	102000	85200	60700
43	137000	122000	104000	87000	61600
44	140000	124000	106000	88700	62500
45	142000	126000	108000	90400	63400
46	145000	129000	110000	92100	64300
47	147000	131000	112000	93700	65100
48	150000	133000	114000	95400	65900
49	152000	135000	115000	97000	66700
50	154000	137000	117000	98700	67500
51	157000	139000	119000	100000	68300
52	159000	141000	121000	101000	69100
53	162000	143000	123000	103000	69800
54	164000	144000	124000	105000	70500
55	166000	146000	126000	106000	71200
56	168000	148000	128000	108000	71900
57	171000	150000	129000	109000	72600
58	173000	152000	131000	111000	73300

NCPU	400/8MB	400/4MB	336/4MB	250/4MB	250/1MB
59	175000	154000	133000	112000	74000
60	177000	156000	134000	114000	74600
61	179000	157000	136000	115000	75200
62	181000	159000	138000	117000	75900
63	184000	161000	139000	118000	76500
64	186000	162000	141000	120000	77100

Workgroup Servers

ESTIMATION TABLE A-25 Enterprise 250 / Enterprise 450

NCPU	400/2MB	300/2MB	250/2MB
1	3800	3120	2490
2	7500	6150	4810
4	14300	11700	9360

Desktop Servers

ESTIMATION TABLE A-26 Ultra2 / Ultra60 / Ultra30

NCPU	360/2MB	300/2MB	200/2MB
1	3680	3120	2520
2	6830	5790	4690

ESTIMATION TABLE A-27 Ultra-5 / Ultra-10

NCPU	440/2MB	360/512K	300/512K	266/512K
1	3280	2410	2050	1840

ESTIMATION TABLE A-28 Ultra-1

NCPU	167/512K	143/512K
1	1500	1280

ESTIMATION TABLE A-29 SPARCcenter 2000E / SPARCcenter 2000

NCPU	85/2MB	60/2MB	60/1MB	50/2MB	50/1MB	40/1MB
1	837	770	707	651	451	397
2	1660	1530	1400	1290	898	790
3	2480	2280	2090	1930	1340	1170
4	3290	3020	2780	2560	1770	1560
5	4090	3760	3460	3180	2200	1940
6	4880	4490	4120	3800	2630	2310
7	5660	5210	4790	4410	3050	2690
8	6440	5920	5440	5010	3470	3050
9	7200	6630	6090	5610	3880	3420
10	7960	7320	6730	6200	4290	3780
11	8710	8010	7360	6780	4700	4130
12	9450	8690	7990	7360	5100	4480
13	10100	9370	8610	7930	5490	4830
14	10900	10000	9220	8490	5880	5180
15	11600	10600	9830	9050	6270	5520
16	12300	11300	10400	9600	6650	5850
17	13000	11900	11000	10100	7030	6190
18	13700	12600	11600	10600	7400	6520
19	14400	13200	12100	11200	7770	6840
20	15000	13800	12700	11700	8140	7160

ESTIMATION TABLE A-30 SPARCserver 1000E / SPARCserver 1000

NCPU	85/1MB	60/1MB	50/1MB	40/1MB
1	662	623	441	387
2	1280	1210	829	724
3	1880	1770	1170	1010
4	2430	2310	1470	1270
5	2960	2810	1730	1490
6	3460	3290	1960	1680
7	3930	3750	2170	1850
8	4380	4190	2350	2000

ESTIMATION TABLE A-31 SPARCstation 20

NCPU	75/1MB	60/1MB	50/1MB	50 no E$
1	638	530	402	290
2	1230	1020	782	563
4			1480	

ESTIMATION TABLE A-32 SPARCstation 10

NCPU	50/1MB	40/1MB	40
1	338	284	204
2	657	552	397
4	1240		

ESTIMATION TABLE A-33 SPARCstation 2, SPARCstation IPX

NCPU	40/64K
1	149

References

Sun BluePrints OnLine Articles

The following Sun BluePrints OnLine articles are available at:

http://www.sun.com/software/solutions/blueprints/browsesubject.html

System Management

An Overview of Methodology (4/99) by Adrian Cockcroft

Presents an in-depth overview of service level definitions and interactions and the resource management control loop.

Dynamic Reconfiguration (4/99) by Enrique Vargas

Provides the fundamentals of DR.

Managing NFS™ Workloads (4/99) by Richard McDougall, Adrian Cockcroft, and Evert Hoogendoorn

Demonstrates the use and management of NFS.

Solaris Resource Manager™ (4/99) by Richard McDougall

Presents an overview and examples of SRM software functions.

Solaris Resource Manager™ – Decay Factors and Parameters (4/99) by Richard McDougall

Discusses SRM software, with emphasis on decay factors and parameters.

Solaris Resource Manager™ – Decay and Scheduler Parameters (4/99) by Richard McDougall

Continues with the topic of the SRM software decay factor.

Solaris™ Bandwidth Manager (6/99) by Evert Hoogendoorn

Explains the benefits of the SBM software.

Load Sharing Facility (6/99) by Tom Bialaski

Describes how a LSF can be used as a resource management tool for running technic batch applications such as simulations.

Dynamic Reconfiguration Requirements for I/O Device Drivers (6/99) by Enrique Varga

Covers the device driver functions that are required to fully support the DR framework.

Starfire™ Server DR-Detach and DR-Attach Requirements (8/99) by Enrique Vargas

Provides a complete list of Starfire server prerequisites for enabling attach and detac operations on any system board.

Modelling the Behavior of SRM Software (8/99) by Dr. Neil Gunther, Richard McDouga and Adrian Cockcroft.

Discusses how the SRM software achieves dynamic resource consumption by using fair-share CPU scheduling algorithm.

SRM: Resource Assignment (8/99) by Richard McDougall

Explains how users are assigned resource lnodes and under what circumstances they change to ensure that resource limits are allocated correctly.

Policy-Based Networks (10/99) by Jean-Christophe Martin

Discusses the network policy concept in greater depth, and shows how it is implemented in the SBM software.

Processing Accounting Data into Workloads (10/99) by Adrian Cockcroft

Provides information about Solaris OE system accounting and includes code example that extract the data in a usable format and pattern-match it into workloads.

Observability (12/99) by Adrian Cockcroft

Discusses capacity planning and performance management techniques.

Scenario Planning - Part 1 (02/00) by Adrian Cockcroft

Discusses scenario planning techniques to help predict future demands. Part 1 explains how to simplify your model down to a single bottleneck.

Scenario Planning - Part 2 (03/00) by Adrian Cockcroft

Presents Part 2 of the *Scenario Planning* article and explains how to follow up a simple planning method based on a spreadsheet that is used to break down a problem and experiment with alternative future scenarios.

Sun BluePrints Series

Other relevant Sun BluePrints books include:

- *Resource Management* by Richard McDougall, Adrian Cockcroft, Evert Hoogendoorn, Enrique Vargas, Tom Bialaski, Sun Press/Prentice Hall, 1999, ISBN 0-13-025855-5

  Demonstrates how to manage system resources to meet system and performance service levels. The theory of resource management is introduced, and a detailed analysis of what is required to implement resource management in the Solaris OE is explored. In addition, *Resource Management* includes examples of typical system workloads and describes how the SRM facilities and products can be used with these workloads. These workloads include databases, file services, Web servers, batch tasks, and ISP configurations.

- *Solaris™ Guide for Windows NT Administrators* by Tom Bialaski, Sun Press/Prentice Hall, 1999, ISBN 0-13-025854-7

  Describes a method by which experienced Windows NT administrators can leverage their networking expertise to quickly get up-to-speed on Solaris OE administration. The book covers all important aspects of Windows NT and Solaris OE integration, including file, print, email, and Web services.

- *Solaris™ PC Netlink: Performance Sizing and Deployment* by Don DeVitt, Sun Press/Prentice Hall, 2000, ISBN 0-13-026686-8

  Provides information that enables system planners and administrators to install, tune, and use their Solaris PC NetLink server to its maximum functionality and performance. This book includes information to help system planners scale their Solaris PC NetLink server to their own PC client environment.

- *Backup and Restore Practices For Sun Enterprise™ Servers* by Stan Stringfellow and Miroslav Klivansky with Michael Barto, Sun Press/Prentice Hall, 2000, ISBN 0-13-089401-X

Discusses backup and restore best practices and is a practical guide for IT organizations that are tasked with implementing or revamping a backup/restore architecture. The book includes case studies, a methodology, and example runbooks. It addresses issues such as scalability and performance of the backup restore architecture, criteria for selecting tools and technologies, and trade-offs that must be considered. The book provides technical guidelines for planning the architecture to meet service levels, as well as general advice and guidance.

SunPS Information and Web Sites

- Sun Professional Services: http://www.sun.com/service/sunps/
- SunWorld Online: http://www.sunworld.com/

Web Sites for Performance Tools

- BMC Corporation for Best/1 and Patrol: http://www.bmc.com
- SES simulation sofware: http://www.ses.com
- TeamQuest Corporation: http://www.teamquest.com
- The SAS Institute: http://www.sas.com

Other Related Books

- *Capacity Planning for Web Performance* by D. A. Menasce and B. Almeida, Prentice Hall, 1998, ISBN: 0136938221
- *Configuration and Capacity Planning for Solaris™ Servers* by Brian Wong, Sun Press Prentice Hall, 1997, ISBN: 0133499529
- *The Practical Performance Analyst* by Dr. Neil Gunther, iUniverse.com, 1997, ISBN: 059512674X
- *Performance Analysis of Transaction Systems* by W. H. Highleyman, Prentice Hall, 1989, ASIN: 0136570089
  Recommended if you are looking for more detailed analytical methods to analyze database systems.

- *Performance Engineering of Software Systems* by Connie U. Smith, Addison-Wesley, 1991; also: http://www.perfeng.com, ASIN: 0201537699
  This book should be required reading for managers of software development organizations. It describes a detailed method for engineering performance into applications from the beginning, rather than trying to fix them afterwards. A performance engineering tool called SPE.ED and training classes are also available.

- *Practical Queueing Analysis* by M. Tanner, Prentice Hall, 1994, ISBN: 0079121098

- *Sun Performance and Tuning – Java and the Internet (2nd Edition)* by Adrian Cockcroft and Richard Pettit, Sun Press/Prentice Hall, 1998, ISBN: 0130952494

- *The Art of Computer System Performance Analysis* by Raj Jain, Wiley, 1991, ISBN: 0471503363
  This is one of the best in-depth books on performance analysis and capacity planning techniques.

- *Web Performance Tuning* by Patrick Killelea, O'Reilly, 1998, ISBN: 1565923790

Glossary

access control list	(ACL) A file that specifies which users can access a particular resource, such as a file system.
accounting	Keeping track of resource usage on a machine. The Solaris Resource Manager (SRM) software provides accounting features.
ACL	See *access control list*.
administration tool	A graphical user interface (GUI) tool for configuring the Solaris Bandwidth Manager (SBM) software.
administrative domain	A collection of network elements under the same administrative control and grouped together for administrative purposes.
ADOP	See *automatic degree of parallelism*.
alarm	The means by which notification is sent when an exception occurs.
alternate pathing	(AP) A software mechanism that works in conjunction with dynamic reconfiguration (DR) to provide redundant disk and network controllers and their respective physical links. The main purpose of AP is to sustain continuous network and disk I/O when system boards are detached from a machine or dynamic system domain, or DSD (in the case of the Starfire) that is running a live copy of the Solaris operating environment (OE).
AP	See *alternate pathing*.
application resource measurement	(ARM) A means of measuring the end-to-end response time of a system.
ARM	See *application resource measurement*.
ASE	Sybase Adaptive Server Enterprise.
attaching	See *DR (dynamic reconfiguration) attach*.

automatic degree of parallelism   (ADOP) A feature of the Oracle8*i* Database Resource Manager that attempts optimize system utilization by automatically adjusting the degree of parallelism for parallel query operations.

backfilling   The execution of a job that is short enough to fit into the time slot during which the processors are reserved, allowing for more efficient use of the available resources. Short jobs are said to backfill processors reserved for larg jobs.

BBSRAM   Boot bus static random access memory.

blacklist   A file that enables you to specify components, such as system boards, that should not be configured into the system. The blacklist file is read and processed at startup.

BMC Best/1   BMC Software's Best/1 products provide tools to address performance management requirements across OS/390, Parallel Sysplex, SAP R/3, UNIX, Windows NT, VM, and AS/400 environments.

CBQ   See *class based queuing*.

CCMS   A tool that provides information to SAP R/3, allowing it to measure the performance of key user transactions and the response time of the back-end database for applications.

CICS   See *customer information control system*.

CIM   See *common information model*.

class-based queuing   (CBQ) The underlying queuing technology used in the Solaris Bandwidth Manager (SBM) software.

classes of service   (CoS) A feature supported by the Solaris Bandwidth Manager (SBM) softwar that allows network traffic to be organized so that urgent traffic gets higher priority than less important traffic.

classifier   A component of the Solaris Bandwidth Manager (SBM) software that allocate packets to a class queue. When a packet arrives, the classifier analyzes the packet protocol, its type of service (ToS) value, URL information, source information, and destination information and allocates the packet to a class queue where it waits to be processed.

CLI   command-line interface, as opposed to graphical user interface (GUI).

cluster   A collection of computers interconnected via a high-speed interface that allov the environment to behave as a single unified computing resource.

clustered cache   A method of caching Web pages where multiple servers use the intercache protocol (ICP) to talk among themselves and form an explicit hierarchy of siblings and parents. If the load would overwhelm a single server or if high availability is important, multiple servers are configured as siblings. Each sibling stores data in its cache, but also uses ICP to search the caches of other siblings.

CMIP A scalable OSI-based network management protocol that is used in situations where Simple Network Management Protocol (SNMP) is not powerful enough.

common information model (CIM) A metamodel based on the unified modelling language (UML) that supplies a set of classes with properties and associations. The CIM provides a conceptual framework within which it is possible to organize information about a managed environment.

control interval In control theory, the rate at which measurements are made and corrections are applied.

CoS See *classes of service*.

cross-system coupling facility (XCF) A Workload Manager (WLM) component that communicates policies, metrics, and control data between Sysplex nodes.

customer information control system (CICS) An interactive transaction processing system from IBM.

DDI_ATTACH A function, used by dynamic reconfiguration, or DR (called from `dr_driver`), that provides the ability to attach a particular instance of a driver without affecting other instances that are servicing separate devices.

DDI_DETACH A function, used by dynamic reconfiguration, or DR (called from `dr_driver`), that provides the ability to detach a particular instance of a driver without affecting other instances that are servicing separate devices.

DDI/DKI Device driver interface/device kernel interface. These are function call entry points that device drivers should implement to fully support dynamic reconfiguration (DR). DDI/DKI is specified in the "Writing Device Drivers" section of the *Driver Developer Site 1.0 AnswerBook* (*http://docs.sun.com*).

DDI_RESUME A function, used by dynamic reconfiguration, or DR (called from `dr_driver`), that provides the ability to detach a board that contains the kernel cage (OBP OpenBoot PROM), kernel, and non-pageable memory). The kernel cage can only be relocated after all of the drivers throughout the entire dynamic system domain, or DSD (not just on the board being detached) are quiesced to guarantee the data integrity of the kernel cage relocation. `DDI_RESUME` resumes the drivers after the quiesce period.

DDI_SUSPEND A function, used by dynamic reconfiguration, or DR (called from `dr_driver`), that provides the ability to detach a board that contains the kernel cage (OBP (OpenBoot PROM), kernel, and non-pageable memory). The kernel cage can only be relocated after all of the drivers throughout the entire dynamic system domain, or DSD (not just on the board being detached) are quiesced to guarantee the data integrity of the kernel cage relocation. DDI_SUSPEND suspends the drivers to begin the quiesce period.

decay   The period by which historical usage is discounted.

DEN   The Directory Enabled Networks working group. The goal of this group is to offer a standard information model and directory schemas to tie together use and applications with network elements, protocols, and services through specific relationships. By complying to this information model and the DEN schemas, different network equipment and application vendors should be ab to build interoperable network elements around a central directory.

detaching   See *DR (dynamic reconfiguration) detach.*

Diff-Serv   The Differentiated Services (Diff-Serv) working group of the Internet Engineering Task Force (IETF). Diff-Serv addresses network management issues related to end-to-end quality of service (QoS) within diverse and complex networks.

DIMM   Dual in-line memory module. A memory module with a higher capacity and faster performance than a SIMM (single in-line memory module). It is current used as the memory source for all Sun Microsystems platforms.

direct control   A means of control that operates on the resource you want to control. For example, the Solaris Resource Manager (SRM) software controls CPU usage per user by implementing a scheduling class that decides who should get wh share of the CPU.

DISC   Dynamic internal service class created by the Workload Manager (WLM). These classes enable the WLM to manage transactions. Each DISC is associate with one or more normal service classes and a given server component. The number of transactions using each route then allows the DISCs to be weighte Thus, if the external or standard service class goal is not being met, the associated DISCs can be managed (if that is where a bottleneck lies).

distributed queuing system   A batch system product from Florida State University that is available in the public domain. The set of system resources it understands is host (by name) system architecture, operating system type, amount of memory, and CPU usage.

DMTF   Desktop Management Task Force.

DQS   See *distributed queuing system.*

DR   See *dynamic reconfiguration.*

DR attach   The process of bringing a system board under the control of the Solaris operating environment (OE) through use of the dynamic reconfiguration (D mechanism.

DR detach	The process of removing a system board from Solaris operating environment (OE) control through use of the dynamic reconfiguration (DR) mechanism.
DSD	See *dynamic system domains.*
DSS	Decision support system.
DSS/DW	Decision support system/data warehousing.
dynamic reconfiguration	(DR) A Sun Microsystems technology supported on the Starfire and other Sun Enterprise servers which allows system boards to be added (attached) or removed (detached) from a single server or domain.
dynamic system domain	(DSD) A Starfire independent hardware entity formed by the logical association of its system boards. Each domain on the Starfire enjoys complete hardware isolation from other domains, executes its own private version of the Solaris operating system, and is centrally managed by the system service processor (SSP).
ELIM	See *extended load information manager.*
Enterprise 10000	See *Sun Enterprise 10000.*
ERP	Enterprise resource planning.
error event	A discrete on/off event, as opposed to a continuous variable to be compared against a limit.
exception	A condition that represents a problem in processing a job. The load sharing facility (LSF) can watch for several types of exception conditions during a job's life cycle.
exclusive scheduling	A type of scheduling used by the load sharing facility (LSF) that makes it possible to run exclusive jobs on a host. A job only runs exclusively if it is submitted to an exclusive queue. An exclusive job runs by itself on a host. LSF does not send any other jobs to the host until the exclusive job completes.
Extended Load Information Manager	(ELIM) The load sharing facility (LSF) uses the Load Information Manager (LIM) as its resource monitoring tool. To modify or add load indices, an ELIM can be written.
fairshare	A form of scheduling used by the load sharing facility (LSF) to prevent a single user from using up all the available job slots, thus locking out other users. Fairshare scheduling is an alternative to the default first come, first served scheduling. Fairshare scheduling divides the processing power of the LSF cluster among users and groups to provide fair access to resources for all jobs in a queue. LSF allows fairshare policies to be defined at the queue level so that different queues can have different sharing policies.

FlowAnalyzer (NetFlow)	An application that uses the output from NetFlow FlowCollector. It provides very elaborate processing, graphing, and reporting options that can be used f network analysis, planning, troubleshooting, and more
FlowCollector (NetFlow)	A NetFlow datagram consumer for one or more NetFlow devices. These devices simply point to the host and port number on which the FlowCollect software is running. The FlowCollector aggregates this data, does preprocessing and filtering, and provides several options to save this data tc disk (such as flat files). Other applications such as network analyzing, planning, and billing can use these files as input.
Gigaplane-XB	The interconnect on the Starfire that provides main memory access through point-to-point data router which isolates data traffic between system boards and minimizes any performance degradation when memory interleaving is disabled.
goal	Goal-based policies are prescriptitive rather than reactive. A goal can be translated into a mixture of limits, priorities, and relative importance levels. Goals can include actions to be performed when the goal cannot be met.
Health Monitor	See *SyMON Health Monitor*.
heavily damped	A system is heavily damped if you feed back a small proportion of an error over a longer control interval. A heavily damped system tends to be sluggis and unresponsive when a large time constant is used.
hierarchical fairshare	A method of sharing resources, supported by the load sharing facility (LSF). Hierarchical fairshare enables resources to be allocated to users in a hierarchical manner. Groups of users can collectively be allocated a share, ar that share can be further subdivided and given to subgroups, resulting in a share tree.
host-based resources	Resources that are not shared among hosts, but are tied to individual hosts. / application must run on that host to access such resources. Examples are CP memory, and swap space. Using up these resources on one host does not affe the operation of another host.
Hostview	A graphical user interface (GUI) program that runs on the system service processor (SSP) machine (which is a component of an Enterprise 10000 system Hostview enables you to monitor and control an Enterprise 10000. For example, Hostview can display continuous readouts of power and temperatu levels at various locations within the Enterprise 10000 server.
HPC	High-Performance Computing.
HP OpenView	Computer-oriented local and wide area networks are normally managed usir the Simple Network Management Protocol (SNMP) with Solstice SunNet Manager or HP OpenView products collecting and displaying the data. Both products provide some visibility into what is happening in the computer

systems on the network, but they are focused on network topology. Resource management is done on a per-network basis, often by controlling the priority of data flows through intelligent routers and switches.

HTTP Hypertext transfer protocol. HTTP is used by Web servers to host content and respond to HTTP requests from Web browsers.

IBM Workload Manager (WLM) A comprehensive toolset for MVS that provides an automated resource management environment, driven by high-level business goals, and that, in many cases, is self-tuning. Tools are provided to define the business goals or objectives, to control system resources, and to feed metrics concerning these resources back to the resource controller, which attempts to ensure that the goals are met.

IETF Internet Engineering Task Force.

indirect control A means of control that works via resources that are dependent upon the resource that is being controlled. For example, to limit the I/O throughput of a process, it is sufficient to be able to measure the I/O throughput and limit the CPU resources for that process.

intercache protocol (ICP) A protocol used to implement clustered caches. (See *clustered cache*.)

interleaving See *memory interleaving*.

intimate shared memory (ISM) A way of allocating memory so that it can't be paged. The shared memory area is often the largest component of a database's memory requirements, and is the easiest to insulate between database instances. Because intimate shared memory is wired down, the memory allocated to each database instance stays allocated and one instance cannot steal memory from another.

Int-Serv The Integrated Services working group of the Internet Engineering Task Force (IETF).

IP Internet Protocol. IP is the foundation of the TCP/IP architecture. It operates on the network layer and supports addressing. IP enables data packets to be routed.

ISM See *intimate shared memory*.

ISP Internet service provider; a company that provides point-of-presence access to the Internet.

ISPF Interactive system productivity facility; a generic MVS interface that can be used by the operator/administrator to define, activate, and deactivate policies.

Java Dynamic Management Kit A JavaBeans based framework for developing and deploying dynamic management based applications. Autonomous agents can be deployed in rea time to perform management tasks for devices on the network.

Java Virtual Machine (JVM) The machine image, implemented in software, upon which Java code runs.

JTAG Joint Test Action Group, IEEE Std. 1149.1. JTAG is an alternate communicatio interface between the system service processer (SSP) machine and Enterpris 10000 server, and is used when the standard network connection between th SSP and Enterprise 10000 is unavailable.

JVM See *Java Virtual Machine*.

kernel cage A special data structure (normally contained within a single system board) th controls the dynamic growth of all nonrelocatable memory, including the OpenBoot PROM (OBP) and kernel memory. When dynamic reconfiguration (DR) is used to detach a system board containing the kernel cage, it is necessary to quiesce the operating system to ensure that no I/O or kernel activity occurs while the kernel cage is being relocated.

kernel memory Memory that is used to run the operating system.

kernel module A Solaris Bandwidth Manager (SBM) software module that contains the *classifier* and *scheduler*.

LAN See *local area network*.

lightly damped If you feed back a large proportion of an error with a short control interval, t system is said to be lightly damped. A lightly damped system is very responsive to sudden changes, but will probably oscillate back and forth.

LIM See *Load Information Manager*.

limit A simple rule with a single input measurement. It is also common to have several thresholds with a warning level action and a critical problem level action for the same measure.

lnode Limit node; a node in a special resource tree used by the Solaris Resource Manager (SRM) software. The SRM is built around lnodes, which are a fundamental addition to the Solaris kernel. Lnodes correspond to UNIX UID (user IDs), and may represent individual users, groups of users, application and special requirements. The lnodes are indexed by UID and are used to record resource allocations policies and accrued resource usage data by processes at the user, group of users, and application levels.

Load Information Manager (LIM) The resource monitoring tool used by the load sharing facility (LSF). The LIM process running on each execution host is responsible for collecting load information. The load indices that are collected include: host status, length of run queue, CPU utilization, paging activity, available swap space, available memory, and I/O activity.

load sharing facility (LSF) A software facility that provides the capability of executing batch and interactive jobs on a pool of networked computers. The Sun Microsystems High-Performance Computing (HPC) package includes the LSF as a vehicle for launching parallel applications on an HPC cluster. In addition to starting batch jobs, the LSF also provides load balancing.

local area network (LAN) A set of computer systems in relatively close proximity that can communicate by means of networking hardware and software.

LPAR Logical Partitions; an IBM S/390™ logical entity that runs its own operating system instance and allocated resources and is managed by Processor Resource/Systems Manager (PR/SM™).

LSF See *load sharing facility.*

LWP Lightweight process.

management information base (MIB) A database that contains network management variables and can be accessed via Simple Network Management Protocol (SNMP).

master host The node where the load sharing facility (LSF) batch queues reside. When the LSF software initializes, one of the nodes in the cluster is elected to be the master host. This election is based on the order of nodes listed in a configuration file. If the first node listed in the configuration file is inoperative, the next node is chosen, and so forth.

maximum bandwidth The amount of spare bandwidth allocated to a class by the Solaris Bandwidth Manager (SBM) software. The maximum bandwidth is dependent on the percentage of bandwidth the class can borrow.

MDF Multiple Domain Facility™; an Amdahl Corporation™ technology that provides logical partitioning for its mainframes. By integrating special hardware for each logical partition or domain, Amdahl processor complexes could run multiple operating systems at close to native performance.

mean value approximation package (MVAP) A solver tool used with TeamQuest to predict system resource utilization, response times, and queue delays in new system models.

memory interleaving	A method of using computer memory that helps increase memory subsystem performance by reducing the probability of hot spots or contention in a few memory banks. This is accomplished by spreading access to multiple memory banks.
Message-passing interface	(MPI) An industry-standard interface used to parallelize applications.
MIB	See *management information base*.
microstate accounting	A method of accounting for resource usage where a high-resolution timestamp is taken on every state change, every system call, every page fault, and every scheduler change. Microstate accounting provides much greater accuracy than sampled measurements.
MPI	See *message passing interface*.
MTM	See *multi-threaded mode*.
Multi-Threaded Mode	(MTM) A database topology where a single process serves many users.
MVAP	See *mean value approximation package*.
negative feedback	A method of applying feedback to a system where you take the error difference between what you wanted and what you got, and apply the inverse of the error to the system to reduce the error in the future.
NetFlow	A product from Cisco that is supported by the Solaris Bandwidth Manager (SBM) software. NetFlow allows for detailed network measurements that can be sent to other software packages, which can process and analyze the data.
Network File System	(NFS) An application that uses TCP/IP to provide distributed file services.
network queuing system	(NQS) A public domain software product that has been enhanced by many hardware vendors. Sterling Software offers a distributed version of NQS called NQS/Exec, which is geared toward a supercomputer environment. Limited load balancing is provided as there is no concept of demand queues, since it uses traditional push queues instead. There is also no control over interactive batch jobs.
NFS	See *Network File System*.
NQS	See *network queuing system*.
NVRAM	Nonvolatile random access memory.
OBP	OpenBoot PROM.
ODS	Informix Online Dynamic Server.

OLTP	Online transaction processing.
operational policy	A policy that is implemented manually as part of operations management. For example, an availability policy can include a goal for uptime and an automatic way to measure and report the uptime over a period. There is no direct control in the system that affects uptime. It is handled by the operations staff.
Oracle8*i* Resource Manager	An Oracle facility that ensures system resources are applied to the most important tasks of the enterprise at the levels required to meet the enterprise goals.
PC NetLink	A product from Sun Microsystems that is based on the AT&T Advanced Server for UNIX. PC NetLink adds functionality that was not previously available on Solaris servers with products such as Samba and SunLink™ PC™ (a.k.a. Syntax TotalNET Advanced Server). PC NetLink adds file and print services, and enables Solaris servers to act as Microsoft Windows NT primary domain controllers (PDCs) or backup domain controllers (BDCs). For enterprises with mixed NT and Solaris Operating Environment (Solaris OE) servers and desktops, Solaris PC NetLink 1.0 offers many new options for utilizing hardware resources and minimizing system administration overhead.
PDP	See *policy decision point*.
PEP	See *policy enforcement point*.
performance index	The ratio of work completed vs. the amount of work that should have been completed to meet the goal.
PIN	See *policy ignorant node*.
platform computing load share facility	See *load sharing facility*.
policy agent	A component of the Solaris Bandwidth Manager (SBM) software that implements the configuration and handles communication with the *kernel module*.
policy control	The application of rules to determine whether or not access to a particular resource should be granted.
policy decision point	(PDP) In policy administration, the point where policy decisions are made.
policy element	A subdivision of policy objects. A policy element contains single units of information necessary for the evaluation of policy rules. Examples of policy elements include the identity of the requesting user or application, user or application credentials, and so forth. The policy elements themselves are expected to be independent of which quality of service (QoS) signaling protocol is used.
policy enforcement point	(PEP) In policy administration, the point where policy decisions are enforced.

policy-ignorant node (PIN) A network element that does not explicitly support policy control usi the mechanisms defined in the applicable standard policy.

policy object An object that contains policy-related information, such as *policy elements*, a is carried in a request or response related to resource allocation decisions.

policy protocol A protocol for communication between the policy decision point (PDP) and policy enforcement point (PEP). The policy protocol can be any combination COPS, Simple Network Management Protocol (SNMP), and Telnet/CLI (command-line interface).

POST Power-ON self test; a suite of hardware diagnostic tests that ensure full functionality of a system board.

preemptive scheduling A method of scheduling where a high-priority job can bump a lower priorit job that is currently running. The load sharing facility (LSF) provides sever resource controls to prioritize the order in which batch jobs are run. Batch jc can be scheduled to run on a first come, first served basis, fair-sharing betwe all batch jobs, and preemptive scheduling.

priority A relative importance level that can be given to the work done by a system part of a policy that prioritizes some activities over others.

priority decay See *process priority decay.*

priority paging A method of implementing a memory policy with different importance fact for different memory types. Application memory is allocated at a higher priority than file system memory, which prevents the file system from steali memory from other applications. Priority paging is implemented in the Sola 7 operating environment (OE).

process measurements Measurements that show the activity of each user and each application.

process memory Memory allocated to processes and applications.

Process Monitor An optional module within Sun Enterprise SyMON that can be used to view the processes on a system. The Process Monitor can also be configured to pattern-match and accumulate all the processes that make up a workload.

processor reservation A method that allows job slots to be reserved for a parallel job until enough slots are available to start the job. When a job slot is reserved for a job, it is unavailable to other jobs. Processor reservation helps to ensure that large parallel jobs are able to run without underutilizing resources.

processor set The set of processors available to a system.

process priority decay A process decay method used by the Solaris Resource Manager (SRM) software, where each process' priority is decayed according to a fixed decay factor at regular intervals (each second).

Project StoreX A technology being developed at Sun to address modern storage issues. Storage is now open for access in a heterogeneous multivendor environment, where multiple server and storage vendors can all be connected over the storage area network (SAN). This is an emerging technology, and tools to manage a SAN are still being developed. Project StoreX is based on a distributed pure Java framework that can run on servers from any vendor, interface to other storage management software, and manage any kind of attached storage.

provider domain When relocating resources between dynamic system domains (DSDs), a "provider domain" is the domain where a system board gets logically detached from to then have it attached to a "receptor domain."

provider DSD Dynamic reconfiguration (DR) on the Starfire allows the logical detachment of a system board from a provider dynamic system domain, or DSD (the DSD from which resources are borrowed) and the logical attachment of the same system board to a receptor DSD (the DSD where loaned resources are applied).

proxy cache A method of caching Web pages. A proxy caching Web server sits between a large number of users and the Internet, funneling all activity through the cache. Proxy caches are used in corporate intranets and at Internet service providers (ISPs). When all the users are active at once, regardless of where they are connecting to, the proxy cache server will get very busy

PR/SM™ Processor Resource/Systems Manager; an IBM S/390 hardware feature that allows customers to statically allocate processor and I/O resources to Logical Partitions (LPARs) to concurrently run multiple operating system instances on the same machine.

QoS See *quality of service*.

quality of service (QoS) A measure of the speed and reliability of a service. The Solaris Bandwidth Manager (SBM) software provides the means to manage your network resources to provide QoS to network users. QoS is a network-wide issue; if congestion takes place anywhere on the network, it affects the overall QoS.

RAS reliability, accessibility, and serviceability.

receptor domain When relocating resources between dynamic system domains (DSDs), a "receptor domain" is the domain that receives a system board after having it logically detached from a "provider domain."

receptor DSD Dynamic reconfiguration (DR) on the Starfire allows the logical detachment of a system board from a provider dynamic system domain, or DSD (the DSD from which resources are borrowed) and the logical attachment of the same system board to a receptor DSD (the DSD where loaned resources are applied).

repository access protocol The protocol used to communicate between a policy repository and the repository client. LDAP is one example of a repository access protocol.

Resource Management Facility	(RMF) A component of the workload manager (WLM) that tracks metrics including progress against goals.
RMF	See *Resource Management Facility*.
RSVP	A protocol (part of the Int-Serv framework) that provides applications the ability to have multiple levels of quality of service (QoS) when delivering da across the network. RSVP provides a way for an application to communicat its desired level of service to the network components. It requires each hop from end to end to be RSVP-enabled, including the application itself (throug an application programming interface, or API). Bandwidth is reserved at ea hop along the way before transmitting begins, guaranteeing that enough resources will be available for the duration of the connection.
SAN	See *storage area network*.
scheduler	A component of the Solaris Resource Manager (SRM) software that schedul users and applications.
scheduler term	The period of time during which the Solaris Resource Manager (SRM) softwa ensures that a particular user or application receives its fair share of resourc
security policy	A type of policy that aims at preventing access to certain resources or allowi designated users to manage subsystems. For example, Sun Enterprise SyMC 2.0 software includes access control lists for operations that change the state a system, and multiple network domain views to give different administrati roles their own view of the resources being managed.
server consolidation	A current trend by data centers to reduce the cost of server ownership by reducing the physical footprint and reducing the number and management cost of multivendor platforms. The basis of server consolidation is to combi applications and data contained in several smaller servers into a single large server.
service class	A class that defines a set of goals, together with periods, duration, and importance. A number of individual processes and CICS/IMS (customer information control system/information management system) transactions c be assigned membership to a service class. They will then become subject to specified goals and constraints, including those imposed by any resource group subscribed to by the class. In essence, this is analogous to the Solaris Resource Manager (SRM) lnode, which effectively defines a resource management policy that can be subscribed to.
Service level agreement	(SLA) A written agreement between system managers and end-users that captures the expectations and interactions between end-users, system managers, vendors, and computer systems. Often, many additional interactions and assumptions are not captured formally.

Service level management	(SLM) The process by which information technology (IT) infrastructure is planned, designed, and implemented to provide the levels of functionality, performance, and availability required to meet business or organizational demands.
service provider	In a network policy, the service provider controls the network infrastructure and may be responsible for the charging and accounting of services.
service time	The time it takes for an I/O device to service a request. This can be complex to measure. For example, with today's disk storage systems, the device driver issues a request, that request is queued internally by the RAID controller and the disk drive, and several more requests can be sent before the first one comes back. The service time, as measured by the device driver, varies according to the load level and queue length and is not directly comparable to the old-style service time of a simple disk drive.
SE Toolkit	A toolkit that can be used to develop customized process monitors. The Solaris software can provide a great deal of per-process information that is not collected and displayed by the ps command or Sun Enterprise SyMON 2.0 software. The data can be viewed and processed by a custom written process monitor. You could write one from scratch or use the experimental scripts provided as part of the SE Toolkit. The SE Toolkit is a freely available but unsupported product for Solaris systems. It can be downloaded from http://www.sun.com/sun-on-net/performance/se3.
SEVM	Sun Enterprise Volume Manager; technically equivalent to the Veritas Volume Manager (VxVM).
ShareII	A resource management product from Softway. The Solaris Resource Manager (SRM) software is based on ShareII.
shared resources	A resource that is not tied to a specific host, but is associated with the entire cluster, or a specific subset of hosts within the cluster. Examples of shared resources include: floating licenses for software packages, disk space on a file server which is mounted by several machines, and the physical network connecting the hosts.
SHR Scheduler	A component of the Solaris Resource Manager (SRM) that controls CPU resources. Users are dynamically allocated CPU time in proportion to the number of shares they possess (analogous to shares in a company), and in inverse proportion to their recent usage. The important feature of the SHR Scheduler is that while it manages the scheduling of individual threads, it also portions CPU resources between users.
Simple Network Management Protocol	(SNMP) An open network protocol used by network management systems that are based on TCP/IP.
SLA	See *service level agreement*.
SNIA	Storage Network Industry Association.

SNMP See *Simple Network Management Protocol*.

Solaris Bandwidth Manager (SBM) A product from Sun that provides the means to manage your network resources to provide quality of service (QoS) to network users. It allows network traffic to be allocated to separate classes of service (CoS) so that urgent traffic gets higher priority than less important traffic. Different CoS can be guaranteed a portion of the network bandwidth, leading to more predictable network loads and overall system behavior. Service level agreements (SLAs) can be defined and translated into SBM software controls and policies. Tools and application programming interfaces (APIs) provide an interface for monitoring, billing, and accounting options.

Solaris Management Console (SMC) An application that provides a generic framework for gathering together operating system administration tools and interfacing to industry-standard initiatives such as the Web-based management initiative (WebM) and the common information model (CIM).

Solaris Resource Manager (SRM) A software tool for enabling resource availability for users, groups, and applications. The SRM software provides the ability to allocate and control major system resources such as CPU, virtual memory, and number of processes. The SRM software is the key enabler for server consolidation and increased system resource utilization.

Solstice SunNet Manager Computer-oriented local and wide area networks are normally managed using Simple Network Management Protocol (SNMP), with Solstice SunNet Manager or HP OpenView products collecting and displaying the data. Both products provide some visibility into what is happening in the computer systems on the network, but they are focused on network topology. Resource management is done on a per-network basis, often by controlling the priority of data flows through intelligent routers and switches.

SPARCcluster A highly integrated product line that is focused on improved availability in commercial environments. Its management tools will eventually become an integrated extension to the Sun Enterprise SyMON2.0 software. For High-Performance Computing (HPC), Sun HPC servers use the platform computing load sharing facility (LSF) to perform load balancing on much larger and more loosely coupled clusters.

SRM See *Solaris Resource Manager*.

SRM(IBM) This is the System Resource Manager of the Workload Manager (WLM). The term SRM(IBM) is used in this book to differentiate it from Solaris Resource Manager. SRM(IBM) provides the algorithms for managing resources and caters to dynamic switching between compatibility and goal modes.

SSP	System service processor; Starfire's system administrator and system monitoring interface. The SSP configures the Starfire hardware through a private Ethernet link to create domains. The SSP collects hardware logs, provides boot functions, and produces consoles for each domain.
Starfire	See *Sun Enterprise 10000*.
static resources	Host information that does not change over time, such as the maximum random access memory (RAM) available to processes running on the host.
Storage area network	(SAN) A complex managed storage system, where networked storage using Fibre Channel makes up an interconnection layer between multiple servers or clusters and multiple storage subsystems. A SAN can contain switches and routers just like local or wide area networks, but the protocol in common use is SCSI over Fibre Channel rather than IP over Ethernet. A SAN may also span multiple sites—for example, where remote mirroring is being used for disaster recovery.
StoreX	A technology developed at Sun that enables management of any storage resource in a heterogeneous distributed environment, from storage hardware like devices and switches, to storage software like backup solutions and volume managers. For more information about StoreX, go to: http://www.sun.com/storage/storex/.
submission host	In a typical load sharing facility (LSF) workload configuration, the submission host is the node where the user or operator submits the task to be performed.
Sun Enterprise 10000	A highly scalable 64-processor (UltraSparc II) SMP server with up to 64 GB of memory and over 20 TB of disk space.
Sun Enterprise SyMON 2.0	A product developed by Sun to act as a user interface to hardware features. It is a powerful and extensible system and network monitoring platform that is used to manage other products. Sun Enterprise SyMON 2.0 is a Java-based monitor with multiple user consoles that can monitor multiple systems using the secure extensions to Simple Network Management Protocol version 2 (SNMPv2) to communicate over the network.
Sun Management Center	(SunMC) A product developed by Sun to act as a user interface to hardware features (an upgrade from Sun Enterprise SyMON 2.0). It is a powerful and extensible system and network monitoring platform that can be used to manage other products. SunMC is a Java-based monitor with multiple user consoles that can monitor multiple systems using the secure extensions to Simple Network Management Protocol version 2 (SNMPv2) to communicate over the network.
SunMC	See *Sun Management Center*.
SunNet Manager	See *Solstice SunNet Manager*.
SyMON	See *Sun Enterprise SyMON 2.0*.

SyMON Health Monitor	A SyMON module that can be used in a resource management scenario to determine if a system has enough resources to run comfortably. For example, the CPU state is reported as "red," then either less work or more CPU powe. may be needed on that system. Similarly, if the memory rule reports "red," then the system may need more memory.
system level measurements	A type of measurement. System level measurements show the basic activity and utilization of the memory system and CPUs. Some network measuremen such as TCP/IP throughput are also available on a per-system basis. Per-process activity can be aggregated at a per-system level, then combined with network measurements to measure distributed applications.
Teamquest	A workload analysis product. For more information, go to www.teamquest.com.
time constant	In control theory, the rate at which a system responds to changes.
TNF	See *trace normal form*.
ToS	See *type of service*.
trace normal form	(TNF) A format used to implement tracing (which makes it possible to trace the execution steps of user and kernel processes). Trace normal form, which supported by the Solaris Operating Environment (Solaris OE), provides a sel describing trace output format. TNF allows data structures to be embedded i the trace file without the need for an external definition of their types and contents.
type of service	(ToS) A header field contained in IP packets. Its purpose is to convey information about how the packet should be routed. The Solaris Bandwidth Manager (SBM) software can use this information when classifying a packet. can also change the information, to influence how the packet is routed.
UDB	DB2 Universal Database.
usage decay	A form of decay used by Solaris Resource Manager (SRM) software. The user scheduler is the most important and visible portion of the SRM software and implements usage decays which control long-term CPU allocation responsiveness.
virtual memory	A type of memory that is allocated from a central resource pool and is consumed by an application when it requests memory from the operating system. Virtual memory is not directly related to physical memory usage, because virtual memory is not always associated with physical memory. For example, if an application requests 16 MB from the operating system, the operating system will create 16 MB of memory within that application's address space, but will not allocate physical memory to it until that memory i read from or written to.

virtual Web hosting A Web server configuration where a single server is configured to respond to hundreds or thousands of Internet addresses. Virtual Web hosting is often used in situations where Web sites receive little or no activity most of the time. In these situations, it is usually too expensive to dedicate a single computer system to each Web site.

WAN See *wide area network.*

WebM Web-based management initiative.

wide area network (WAN) A network that provides connectivity across a large geographical area.

WLM See *IBM Workload Manager.*

Workload Manager See *IBM Workload Manager.*

XCF See *cross-system coupling facility.*

Index

sar, 32, 77, 142, 143
vmstat, 32, 77, 78
vxstat, 143
communication ports
parallel, 149
serial, 149
complex disk subsystems, 96
Computer Measurement Group, 58
concatenated disks, 108
Configuration & Service Tracker (CST), 150
configuration inventory, 7
consolidating servers, 146
consolidating workloads, 42
controller capacity, 113
corporate intranet, 147
correlation analysis, 118
CPE, 153
CPU cache/code efficiency, 85
CPU usage, 68
application, 69
CPU utilization, 26
cron command, 142
cross-calls (xcal), 143
CST (Configuration & Service Tracker), 150

D

deltas, 9
device driver, 99
diagnostic testing, 149
diagnostic tests, 150
disk drives, 149
disk measurement, 96
dynamic system domains, 43

E

efficiency variations, 68
electronic commerce, 3
Enterprise 10000, 43
dynamic system domains, 43
Envive Corp, 141
escalation, 27

Examination Institute of the Netherlands (EXIN), 20
example support costs, 37
EXIN (Examination Institute of the Netherlands), 20
exponential growth, 60
user activity, 61

F

fast write cache, 116
fat stripe disks, 108
FC-AL drive, 97
FC-AL interface, 116
FCAPS, 16
field replaceable unit (FRU), 150
finite resource consumption, 86
Foglight Software RAPS, 152
four-phase approach, 6
FRU (field replaceable unit), 150
functional diagnostic testing, 149

G

Gartner Group's TCO tool, 39
ge, 77

H

hard partitioning, 146
hardware health checks, 149
hardware layer, 5
hardware RAID, 97
hardware upgrades, 70
HBA (Host Bus Adapter), 97
health monitoring, 25
hme, 77
Host Bus Adapter (HBA), 97
HP OpenView, 32
http://access1.sun.com/Products/solaris/cst/, 150
HTTP protocol, 143

campaign, 65
MASF (multivariate adaptive statistical filtering), 47, 152
measurement frames, 78
memory, 149
middleware server, 151
mirrored disks, 107
mpstat, 32, 143
multiple systems, tracking, 118
multiprocessor environment, 82
Multi Router Traffic Grapher (MRTG), 130, 140
multivariate adaptive statistical filtering (MASF), 47, 152
mutex calls (smtx), 143
M-value process, 81
MXG Toolset, 153

N

netstat, 32
    command, 142, 143
netstat -k hme0, 77
netstat -s command, 142
network interfaces, 149
network operation center (NOC), 32
NFS server, 103
NOC (network operation center), 32
NVRAM, 116
nx.se script, 77

O

observability
    CPU activity metrics, 143
    network interface statistics, 142
    sar data, 142
    TCP network statistics, 142
    volume manager information, 143
    Web server access logs, 143
OLTP (online transaction processing), 78, 95
online testing, 149
online transaction processing (OLTP), 78, 95
operating system layer, 5

Orca, 130
orcollator.se script, 143

P

paging rates, 26
payroll system, 40
Peoplesoft, 82
percollator.se script, 143
performance factor - P, 113
performance management, 3, 152
performance tools, 130
Platform Computing Corporation, 148
    Load Sharing Facility (LSF), 148
primary bottlenecks, 49
priority_paging, 77
problem reporting, 27
processors, 149

Q

qfe, 77
QoS (quality of service), 147
quality of service (QoS), 147
quantifying capacity, 41

R

RAID, 96
RAID disk subsystem, 103
RAID5
    cached, 111
    large requests, 110
    small requests, 109
RAPS, 152
RAS (reliability, availability, and serviceability), 1●
read prefetch clustering, 105
reliability, availability, and serviceability (RAS), 1●
Resolute Software, 152
resource consumption, 5, 86
resource management, 43

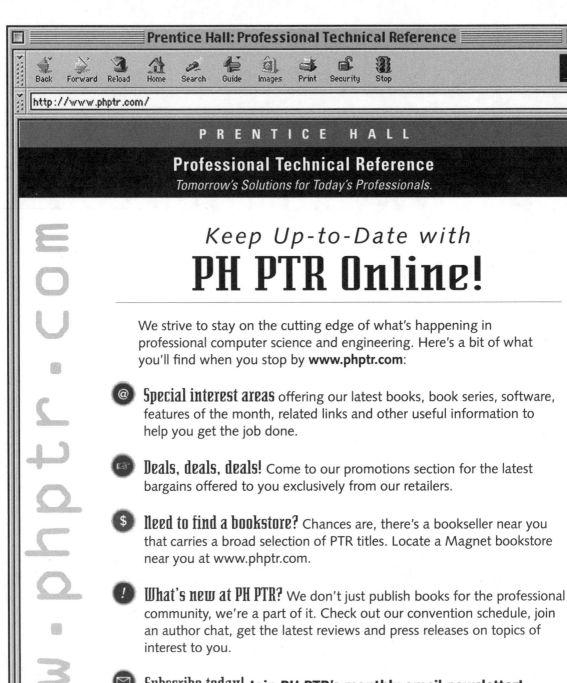